# Shops and Shopping on the Internet

## A practical guide to online stores, catalogues, retailers and shopping malls

GW00686356

# Internet Handbooks

*Other titles in preparation*

# Shops and Shopping

## on the internet

A  practical guide to online stores,
catalogues, retailers and shopping malls

**Kathy Lambert**

**www.internet-handbooks.co.uk**

Copyright © 2000 by International Briefings Ltd

First published in 2000 by Internet Handbooks, a Division of International Briefings Ltd, Plymbridge House, Estover Road, Plymouth PL6 7PY, United Kingdom.

| | |
|---|---|
| Customer services tel: | (01752) 202301 |
| Orders fax: | (01752) 202333 |
| Customer services email: | cservs@plymbridge.com |
| Distributors web site: | www.plymbridge.com |
| Internet Handbooks web site: | www.internet-handbooks.co.uk |

Note: The contents of this book are offered for the purposes of general guidance only and no liability can be accepted for any loss or expense incurred as a result of relying in particular circumstances on statements made in this book. Readers are advised to check the current position with the appropriate authorities before entering into personal arrangements.

Case studies in this book are entirely fictional and any resemblance to real persons or organisations is entirely coincidental.

Printed and bound by The Cromwell Press Ltd, Trowbridge, Wiltshire.

# Contents

# Contents ...............................................................

# List of illustrations

# Preface

In the last couple of years, a staggering number of new electronic shops and stores has been launched on the internet. But what are they like? Where can you find your favourite brands and stores? What about deliveries at home or overseas? Can you safely pay by credit card? This book will take you quickly to all the specialist stores, well-known chains, virtual shopping malls, online auctions rooms, catalogues and freebies of your choice. You will be able to compare prices, and shop till you drop for books, magazines, music, videos, clothes, holidays, electrical goods, games and toys, wines, and a vast array of other goods and services.

According to Euromarc Research, the number of people shopping online has been been doubling every six months. About two thirds of all purchases are for under £50. The most frequent buys are computer hardware and software, books, CDs, travel tickets, holiday packages and clothing. Many more internet users are now prepared to disclose their credit card details on the internet.

More and more people are now basing their purchasing decisions primarily on the information they find on the internet, in particular on web pages. They are looking for detailed product or service information, price and availability, security and reliability. To a lesser extent they find information by clicking on banner advertising, using search engines, and entering discussion forums such as Usenet newsgroups and internet mailing lists. Personal word-of-mouth recommendations seem to play a less significant role.

In comparison to non-connected shoppers, online shoppers spend more on DIY goods, cars, books, pet supplies, toys, CDs and videos, and electronic equipment such as computers, printers, and mobile phones. Higher spending patterns are also emerging in areas such as baby care products, books and magazines, bottled water, breakfast foods, gardening, hosiery, juices and drinks, nappies, pasta, personal care and beauty products, prepared foods, ready-made sauces, records, tapes and sporting goods.

Through continued research, more is becoming known about how people regard online shopping. For example, the main reason for shopping online is the convenience factor. People lead increasingly busy and complicated lives, and have less time to waste on slow and unreliable bus services, driving, traffic jams, parking, standing in queues, and carrying products from store to car park, and from car to home. This factor is closely followed by the good availability of product information on the web. Another key advantage of buying online, reported by more than half of all shoppers, was the absence of pressure from sales people. Males still slightly outnumber females in ordering products or services using the web.

Of course, online shopping has its drawbacks too. The main reasons why purchases are lost are that a particular web site is too slow, the design too confusing, and the web site navigation too complex. These outweigh concerns about credit card security, which has been shown to be a very much lower risk than in the 'real' world.

Internet shopping is here to stay. It looks set to grow at an astronomical rate, fuelled by new developments such as using mobile phones and TV sets for shopping online. Whether you are shopping for yourself, your family or friends, or work in the retail industry, this book should help you take full advantage of this amazing retail revolution.

*Kathy Lambert*

*klambert@internet-handbooks.co.uk*

Fig. 1 – top: the Yahoo! Shopping site is a good example of an online shopping portal, a site that contains a vast number of links to sites of related interest in this case online shops.

Fig. 2 – centre: the main international home page of Buy.Com, one of the best known international shopping sites on the world wide web.

Fig. 3 – bottom: the UK home page of Buy.Com.

# 1 Internet shopping

**In this chapter we will explore:**

▶ *shopping trends on the internet*
▶ *top scams on the internet*
▶ *managing your personal security online*
▶ *shopping tips*
▶ *making your browser secure*
▶ *credit cards for online shopping*
▶ *online currencies and payments systems*
▶ *online consumer services*

## Shopping trends on the internet

*Consumer profiles*

Consumer attitudes towards the internet vary widely. A leading research organisation, Forrester, has produced some interesting comments about internet shopping in Europe, where it surveyed 17,000 households. On-line shopping is still very new, and attitudes of consumers and retailers still being formed. But generally, a much higher proportion of Europeans is expected to adopt a digital lifestyle (http://www.forrester.com).

Net access at home does not necessarily result in online shopping. For example, a proportion of Dutch of households have PCs, but fewer than half have internet access and only 7 per cent of those actually shop on-line. Throughout Europe, only 4 per cent of all households purchased online in the three months prior to the survey; Sweden led with 12 per cent.

Forrester found that the buyer profile mirrors the early online shopper in the US – male, urban, well-educated, and optimistic about technology. Sales are led by fast-moving convenience goods like books, software, and CDs, followed by researched items such as computer supplies. Consumers with longer experience of the internet buy and spend more, typically doubling their spending by their third year. Catalogue shoppers are much more likely to adopt internet shopping than non-catalogue-shoppers.

The overall low penetration of credit cards in Europe – often the only way to buy something online – has hindered online payment activity. How consumers prefer to pay for their purchases, both on- and offline, varies across Europe. In the Netherlands and Sweden, for example, almost half of all online purchases are paid offline, and in Germany almost 20 per cent of people use some other payment method such as a cheque, invoicing, or payment on delivery.

*The rise of online shopping*

Online shopping numbers are small today, but consumers are generally positive about online shopping, and there can be little doubt that online shopping is set to grow very strongly. Consumers need time – a year or two – to gain experience and become comfortable online. The trend to internet access will accelerate this process.

In Europe, product selection remains anaemic, but the next few years will transform this as traditional retailers gradually join the region's first online merchants. With more consumers and retailers coming online, Forrester predicts that the total amount of online business-to-consumer commerce will grow from $2.3 billion in 1999 to $145 billion in 2004.

*Four types of online shopper*
Forrester suggested that there are four types of consumer on the internet:

1. Pioneer Internetters – These have been online for several years and shop there with comfort. They are mostly higher paid and better educated males, who use PCs and other technology at work and in the home. They are career-focused and highly optimistic about technology. They have at least two years' online experience and trust the medium, notably for online financial services.

2. Generation Next – These people have been online less than a year but are already quite active. They are mostly young, sophisticated about technology, and looking for excitement. They are much more focused on entertainment activities like chat and visits to movie and entertainment sites. They are very price aware.

3. Future Buyers – These consumers have been online for under two years and have only just begun to research products online. They are gradually incorporating the net into their lives. This group contains more women than the others. Over the next six months, they plan to shop online, but their trust in the medium remains low and their need for products is only moderate. They have good computing equipment at home, but spend less time online. They much prefer entertainment to financial sites.

4. Shopping Hold-Outs – These constitute more than 40 per cent of all European online consumers. Most have been online for over two years, but have no plans to start shopping in the next six months. They are less experienced with, and less interested in, technology than the other groups. Their trust in the medium is low, and they much prefer to shop in person.

Europe's online population today is still mostly a well-educated, high-income group. However, as the net becomes more representative of the total population, the last two groups are likely to become more mainstream.

In Europe, the UK is expected to see the most dramatic change ahead. Since the profile of British people online is already more mainstream, and their attitude is positive, newcomers online will adopt the net easily, so that online shopping is likely to grow easily there.

The giant US market owes much of its success to the existence of its trusted and stable currency, the dollar, and a long tradition of credit purchasing. Europe – with low trust in the internet and very mixed payment preferences – seems unlikely to see a standard regional payment system emerge in the near future. Europe's banking systems are moving very slowly to cooperate across borders. More Europeans, both consumers and retailers, are becoming used to the US dollar as the *de facto* internet currency.

The early days of net shopping in Europe provoke comparisons with early days in the USA. But as the online population goes mainstream and retailers respond with product diversity, the overall feel of the internet in Europe will become distinctly more European.

## Top scams on the internet

The internet is still a very new medium and there are experienced fraudsters out there keen to exploit the inexperienced newcomer. The risks appear less than those in the real world, but you should always bear them in mind. These are some of the main scams to look out for:

1. Equipment that you ordered online, and paid for, is never delivered, or is of lower quality than you were promised.

2. Pyramid schemes. These offer a chance to invest in an up-and-coming company with a guaranteed high return. You invest, and must ask others to do the same, but when the pyramid collapses, everyone loses, except the person at the top (who has disappeared).

3. Internet-related services that do not involve the delivery of a tangible product. An example could be a hotel or flight booking, some downloadable software (that fails to work), or a promise to design a web site over the internet.

4. Business opportunities or franchises that are claimed to be more profitable than they really are.

5. Work-at-home schemes where you are asked to invest money in start-up services. The problem is, you struggle hard for weeks or months, but never earn enough money to recover your initial outlay.

## Managing your personal security online

Unsecured information sent over the internet can be easily intercepted. That's why you should always use a secure browser, one which will encrypt or scramble purchase information. The two best-known browsers, Internet Explorer and Netscape, both have excellent security features. Few people seem to bother with the security settings in their browsers, simply accepting the default settings, but it is as well to know something about them.

*Making Internet Explorer more secure*
1. Check your security settings. On the main browser toolbar click Tools, Internet Options, then the Security tab. Place it on at least a 'medium' setting. For maximum security, move the slider bar up.

2. Click on the Trusted Sites icon, then Sites. Here you can add the URLs of any sites you completely trust with your personal details.

# Internet shopping ...............................................................

Fig. 4. The security alerts
in the Internet Explorer
browser. The alerts (top
and bottom) show when
you are entering or leaving
a secure web site. When
you are viewing secure
web pages, the little
padlock (centre) will be
closed and feature a
yellow colour.

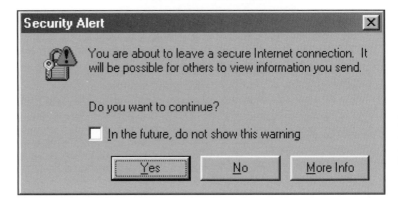

3. On the main browser toolbar click Help, then About Internet Explorer. This will reveal its Cipher Strength. It is probably only 40-bit. To be secure, you should install 128-bit encryption. You can upgrade in a few minutes by visiting: http://windowsupdate.microsoft.com/

4. To find out more, on the main browser toolbar click Help, Contents and Index. Then explore the sections on Sending Information over the Internet Safely, and Protecting Your Computer While You're Online.

*Making Netscape Navigator more secure*
Netscape Navigator can also be made more secure than it is with its normal default settings.

1. The first thing to check is cookies, small text files that can be downloaded to your computer. Online stores may use cookies to store your credit details. The trouble is, other people can view them and so get hold of your details. On the main browser toolbar click Edit, Preferences, then Advanced. Select: 'Accept only cookies that get sent back to the originating server' to stop anyone snatching your private data.

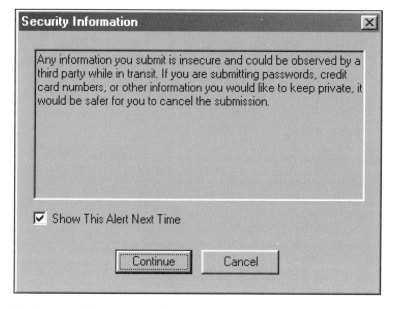

Fig. 5. The security alerts in the Netscape browser. When you are viewing secure web pages, the little padlock (top left) will become closed (top right) and feature a yellow colour. In some versions, a golden key (centre) will appear against a royal blue background. The Netscape Security Information alert (bottom) warns you if a web site is not secure.

2.  On the main browser toolbar click Security, then Navigator (in the left hand column of the window) and make sure all the little security boxes contain a check mark.

3.  To find out more, on the main browser toolbar click Help, then Help Contents, then Security (in the left hand column of the window).

*Looking for secure connections to web sites*
Make sure you're entering your information over a secure connection. More and more leading stores are using state-of-the-art encryption to scramble customer credit card information so that no one else can read it.

It's easy to know when you enter a secure site. First, a reassuring Security Alert will pop up in your browser window. Then, at the bottom of the browser, you will see a small symbol of an unbroken key (Netscape), or a picture of a closed padlock (Internet Explorer). Also, the web address may begin with https (the s means secure). Look out, too, for a blue bar across the very top of your browser window.

If you are unsure whether sensitive information is being transmitted securely, don't send it. If the web site does not have encryption software, consider instead calling its customer services telephone number, faxing your order, or paying by cheque.

# Internet shopping ........................................................

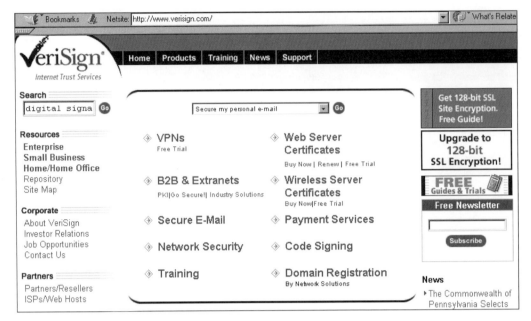

*Obtaining and using a digital signature*

If you want to encrypt any form data or email messages you send in Internet Explorer or Netscape, a digital signature is the answer. Using digital signature encryption ensures that your credit card information cannot be intercepted. Any breach of security would be due to an error by the site to which you had sent your details. Digital signatures are issued by Verisign. To find out more, visit:

http://www.verisign.com/

## Shopping tips

Most people feel rather nervous the first time they go shopping online. In fact, most transactions proceed very smoothly, and online credit card fraud is still surprisingly rare. Here are some important basic tips to help you make sure you don't get your fingers burned.

*Start small*
Consider starting online shopping by buying a book or a CD online.

*Shop around*
Prices vary widely. *Consumer Reports* sent 30 people online shopping, and found that the prices for the same item ranged from $12 to $35 for a white polo shirt and from $18 to $34 for a single computer game. Don't compromise on selection. If you can't find exactly what you want at one site, move on to another. Surf around for sales. Some retailers are beginning to use the internet to clear excess stock or out-of-season goods at big discounts.

*Identify the supplier*
If in any doubt, shop online only with companies you know. Look for the

company's physical location, including its address, post code and phone number. Before making a purchase, call the phone number to make sure. Check the company's credentials with trade organisations or consumer agencies. If you are unfamiliar with the supplier, get hold of its catalogue or brochure so you have some permanent business information in case you need to contact them again. It may pay to check their address in various online yellow pages (see chapter 2). Make a careful note of the merchant's web site address, its uniform resource locator (URL). The URL should indicate that you are dealing with the correct company (e.g. http://www.tesco.co.uk).

*Only buy at secure sites*
To be sure that hackers can't steal your credit card, only shop at secure shopping sites (see above).

*Check out the store's privacy policy before you buy*
When you buy from a site, you don't want your name and buying habits to be sold to the highest bidder, nor do you want to be deluged with junk email ('spam'). Find out what information the site gathers, how it will be used, and whether it shares that information with anyone else. Look in the FAQs, help, or similar areas of a site. Only shop at sites that follow privacy rules from privacy watchdogs such as Truste, the nonprofit group that serves as a watchdog for internet privacy. Truste allows sites to post an online seal if they adhere to Truste's internet privacy policies.

*Protecting your personal information*
When you buy something online, you will usually have to fill out a form first. You may be asked many intrusive questions, such as your annual income, age, phone number and similar information. Don't answer these questions. Many sites put an asterisk* next to questions they require to be answered, so only answer those. If you feel uncomfortable about this, you don't necessarily have to give true information. After all, how would you feel if a shopkeeper asked you similar questions in a high street shop? The shopping site wants your money, and it'll take your money even if you don't give them data surplus to the order fulfilment. Be extremely wary if you are asked to supply national insurance number or bank account details. These should never be required to make a purchase.

*Password accounts*
Some internet sites ask you to create an account with a password. To protect yourself, never use the same password as the one you use for other accounts or sites. Never reveal your password if replying to unsolicited emails, even if they claim to be from your internet service provider. Never give out your internet (log-on) password. No reputable online provider will ever ask for your password other than at first log-on. Change your password often, and be creative. Use a mix of letters and numbers and avoid all common words and names.

*Always pay with a credit card*
When you pay with a credit card, you have a wide variety of consumer

protections – much more than if you pay by cheque or postal order. As an internet consumer you are entitled to all of the rights and benefits given to real world shoppers. Credit card companies are responsible for stolen credit card purchases, and stores are responsible for lost, defective, or damaged merchandise. Pay with plastic, not paper.

*Keep an eye on the latest internet scams*
There are several ways of finding out about internet scams. For example:

1. The US Consumer Gateway reports on internet scams: http://www.consumer.gov

2. The US Federal Trade Commission takes action against internet scamsters, and issues scam warnings: http://www.ftc.gov

3. The US Internet Fraud Watch, run by the National Consumer's League, is another useful source: http://www.fraud.org

4. A good all-round resource is the Scambusters web site: http://www.scambusters.com

*Fig. 7. The well-known Scambuster web site is well worth visiting for its news and updates about various online frauds and fraudsters.*

To date, most problems seem to have arisen at online auction sites.

*Vendor security*
Determine the vendor's level of security. More ecommerce companies are willing to explain their security measures and privacy policies. If you are not comfortable entering your credit card number online, call the company's customer services phone line, or send a fax.

*Terms and conditions*
1. Look for a terms and conditions page and read through it carefully.

2. Find out the company's refund and return policies. A good returns policy will show that the company stands behind its product. Will they refund in full? Is there a time limit on returns? What about postal time? A one-month returns policy is no good if the returned item takes six weeks to reach Australia by surface mail.

3. Pay attention to shipping and handling charges. An online bargain can easily fall apart if you have to pay too much for delivery. Often web merchants don't tell you the cost of shipping and handling until late in the checkout process. Some online merchants pad out their charges by setting the online order default at the more expensive two-day air option. You may need to manually change the setting.

4. Find out the shipping times, and what guarantees are offered about these.

*Perishable goods*
If you are buying perishable goods, look carefully at the shipping information, and prices. Will the company offer a no-quibble replacement, or full refund, if the goods are spoiled on arrival?

*Keeping a record*
Print out a copy of your order and confirmation number for your records. Carefully note the customer ID numbers, electronic invoice numbers, and product descriptions and reference numbers. All this could be useful if you need to contact the business again. You won't be able to complain unless you can prove you are a customer.

*Know your rights*
The same laws that protect you when shopping by phone or post apply when you shop in cyberspace. In most of the developed countries, the law requires that a company must ship your order within the time stated in its advertisements, online or offline. If no time is promised, the company should ship your order within 30 days after receiving it, or give you an 'option notice.' If you do business with a merchant who is subject to different laws, it may prove difficult to resolve a complaint.

*The supplier's past history*
If you are using an American web site, check out the company's reliability report with the Better Business Bureau at:

http://www.bbb.org/

This has business reliability reports online, or you can call, fax, or email a request for information. Close to 2,000 businesses are BBB Online members. Clicking on the BBB Online seal will show the BBB standards met by the company and link you to the company's BBB reliability report.

*Site navigation*
Look for a site that you find easy to navigate. If you find things too difficult or confusing, just leave it. The owner's level of customer service might turn out to be equally difficult and confusing.

*Protecting your privacy*

Every time you buy online, or even just ask for information from a web site, you leave behind a digital trail of valuable information about yourself. Companies are extremely hungry to acquire this, and may be in the business of discreetly buying and selling such information. Look to see that a shopping site you visit has a clear and credible privacy policy. If you don't see one, think twice before doing business with them.

## Credit cards for online shopping

Credit cards are the normal means of paying for your purchases online. However, some sites do give you the option of placing your order by calling a Customer Services phone line, or by sending a fax. All the major credit card companies have their own web sites:

*American Express UK*
http://www6.americanexpress.com/uk/
American Express has launched a credit card with added security features for ecommerce. The first, aimed at allaying shoppers' fears about online transactions, is the American Express Online Wallet. As you would expect, this is a very professional site, attractively designed, functional and fast to download.

*BarclayCard*
http://www6.barclaycard.co.uk/
This is an excellent and informative site. As well as information about its credit card services, there is a useful shopping guide.

*Diners Club*
http://www.dinersclub.com/
From this central site you can visit local Diners Club web sites from numerous countries for information on the card and local services.

*Football MasterCard*
http://www.footballcard.co.uk

*Goldfish MasterCard*
http://www.goldfish.com/

*Graduate MasterCard*
http://www.graduatecard.co.uk
This card is issued in association with the Bank of Scotland. Purchases help support your chosen university, which gets a cut of every transaction (not all universities are included). The service is free to students, provided they pay off the outstanding balance each month. There is no annual charge.

*Judgment Removal Company*
http://www.judgmentremoval.demon.co.uk
JRC are experts in credit repair, removing judgements and defaults from

credit files in the UK. Their testimonials page is worth a look. Services like these are invaluable in helping the private individual fight the bureaucracy of government and big business that threatens to engulf us.

*Marbles*
http://www.marbles.com/
The Marbles card is issued by HFC Bank plc and is only available to people aged 21 or over who are resident in the UK or Channel Islands. Marbles has no annual fee.

*MasterCard*
http://www.mastercard.com
These are the credit card people who started out as Access, using the slogan 'your flexible friend'. The card has since been successfully re-branded, and Mastercard is now universally established. The site, though American, is worth a look. All kinds of online goodies are on offer. There appeared to be no similar European site.

*Visa*
http://www.visa.com
This well presented site has links to products and services, offers and promotions, consumer tips, for businesses, sponsorships and events, new technologies, and about Visa. You can find out how to get a card, organising your holiday money, what to do if your card is lost, and more.

Fig. 8. MasterCard is one of the main credit card providers, and its web site includes lots of practical guidance for shoppers and traders.

*Woolwich Credit Card*
http://www.woolwich.co.uk/creditcard/
A credit card is available from this well-known high-street financial institution. The site consists of fairly basic information.

## Online currencies and payments systems

The internet has seen some interesting recent experiments with virtual currencies. The internet is after all a global environment. How convenient it would be if all transactions could be conducted in one universal currency. There would be no worries then about rates of exchange. In time, more and more people are likely to be earning money over the internet, being paid money over the internet, paying it into internet-based accounts, and then spending the proceeds on the internet. There are huge implications in this for the future of old national currencies and tax-gathering methods. It is too early to predict the ultimate outcome. Perhaps one of type of dollar-based virtual currency will eventually emerge.

*Beenz*
http://www.beenz.com/

Fig. 9. Beenz has developed an online currency. In the longer term, it is possible that such virtual currencies could rival traditional currencies issued by some national governments.

Since 1999, more than a million users have signed up for this 'virtual currency' and conducted some 17 million transactions. One beenz is worth one US cent. Beenz makes its currency available via digital television, mobile phones, personal digital assistants (PDAs) and on video game technology. Beenz is a clear and easy to use web site that allows you to find out where to get beenz and how to spend them. Many web sites also offer beenz as promotional items.

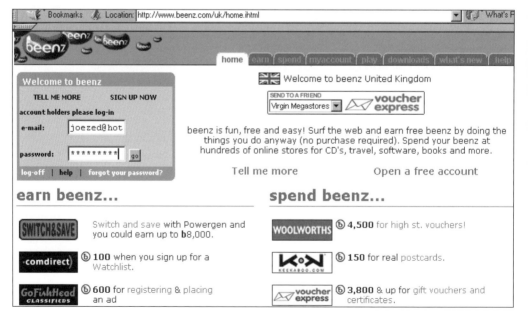

*Ecash*
http://www.digicash.com/
Ecash is a bit like a phone card or a pre-pay mobile phone voucher. It is set to be extended to new technologies, such as internet-ready mobile phones, personal digital assistants and so on. You have to top up your account periodically to make it usable. Ecash (from DigiCash) should not be confused with Ecash Services (below).

*Ecash Services*
http://www.ecashservices.com/
This company offers a similar service to DigiCash (above), though it is mainly geared to the online gambling community. To establish an account you have to give your credit card number, pay in some money, and then draw on that account to pay online shops. Ecash has apparently provided transactions for 100,000 customers.

*I-Points*
http://www.ipoints.co.uk/
I-Points is a British company doing the same kind of thing as Beenz. You shop at certain sites accumulating I-Points, and spend them at affiliated traders. The availability of traders is still limited, but if you want to support a British company, why not take a look.

*Microsoft Wallet*
http://www.microsoft.com
Microsoft Wallet securely stores your address, credit card and other payment details when you shop online. You can find out more from the

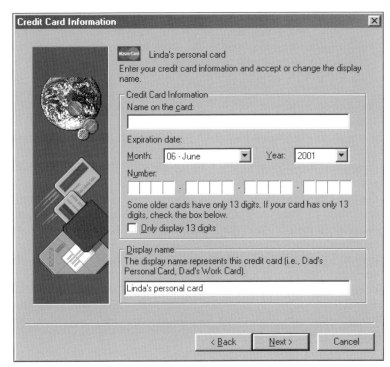

Fig. 10. Why not get yourself a Microsoft Passport Wallet? It will simplify your online shopping.

Microsoft web site, or from the browser Internet Explorer. On the main browser toolbar click Help, then Contents and Index, and in the Index look for Microsoft Wallet.

### Y-Creds
http://www.y-creds.co.uk/
Y-Creds is aimed at the under-18s, who are not allowed to have credit cards. One Y-Cred equates to one penny (UK). The idea is that the parent or guardian opens an account for the young person and tops it up with cash from time to time by credit card, cheque or standing order. The children can then spend the balance rather like a phone card or debit card. Few retailers yet accept this form of payment. However, there is an incentive for kids to nominate other stores. If they are the first to suggest a particular web site, they should receive 10,000 Y-creds in their account – equivalent to £100.

### Yahoo! Wallet
http://wallet.yahoo.com/
Yahoo! Wallet is a service that lets you securely store your credit card information with Yahoo!. It has been devised to enable people to purchase items from the store merchants on Yahoo! Shopping, of which there are now well over 5,000.

## Online consumer services

### British and Irish Ombudsman Association
http://www.bioa.org.uk
This is a free service set up to deal with complaints from ordinary British and Irish citizens, about either public or private sector services. You might be surprised to see how many different ombudsmen there are. The site contains summaries of what they do, email contact addresses, and hyperlinks to the relevant web sites.

### Consumers' Association (Which)
http://www.which.net
This is the online version of the famous series of consumer magazines. It has a product testing section, and some free reports available on the site.

### Consumer World
http://www.consumerworld.org/
Consumer World is a public service, non-commercial site which has gathered over 1,800 sites on useful consumer resources on the internet and categorised them for easy access. This is the site to access if you want information on buying advice and product reviews or if you want to comparison-shop for bargains, file a consumer complaint, find consumer rights booklets or find a low credit card rate. The site offers digests of consumer news, a free email newsletter, details of consumer protection agencies around the world and consumer advice. This is well worth a visit if you want to be aware of your rights as a consumer.

*eSmarts*
http://www.esmarts.com/
eSmarts is a retail information site. It aims to make it easy for you to shop online and get quality products, bargain prices and great service. It publishes reviews and rankings of internet merchants, and has its own shopping guides and links to top shopping sites. It researches the merchants (in various industries), and does extensive independent and objective reviews of these merchants. It then ranks the merchants to make it easy for you to quickly locate the best place to shop for anything you want. You can share your experience (good or bad) and your concerns on its message boards so that others can read and respond.

*Office of Fair Trading*
http://www.oft.gov.uk/
The Office of Fair Trading plays a key role in protecting the economic welfare of consumers, and in enforcing United Kingdom competition policy. On this web site you will find information on the work of the OFT, its annual report, news stories, press releases and articles from *Fair Trading* magazine, reference material for consumer protection and competition policy, and advice on the rights of UK consumers.

*Public Eye*
http://www.thepubliceye.com
PublicEye is an independent service that enables consumers to rate ebusinesses for reliability, privacy and customer satisfaction. Since 1996, its monitoring system has been providing information for consumers, who are then empowered to make confident online buying decisions. This is achieved through a customer satisfaction reporting system.

*Safer Shopper*
http://www.safershopper.com/
Safer Shopper is a gateway to secure shopping. It is a general purpose

Fig. 11. Safe Shopper can guide you towards secure shopping sites, and provide help in making your browser and online shopping experiences more secure.

25

internet shopping resource created to provide safe shopping tips, links to safer shopping sites, and a newsletter with details of bargains and safe shopping information.

### Shop.org
http://www.shop.org/
Founded in 1996, this association serves the needs of retailers that sell goods or services directly to the consumer via the internet. This would be an essential resource for anyone thinking of selling online.

### Times-Money
http://www.times-money.co.uk
This is a UK-based personal finance site run by *The Times* newspaper. It is regularly updated on working days and you should be able to rely on the information it contains.

### Trading Standards
http://www.tradingstandards.gov.uk
This is an official one-stop shop for consumer protection information in the UK. It provides a wealth of information for consumers and businesses, schools, advice and information centres, community organisations, business support agencies and trade associations. You can use the site to contact your local trading standards service for advice and information. Just type your postcode in the box provided and press Find, and you should see a hyperlink to your local office.

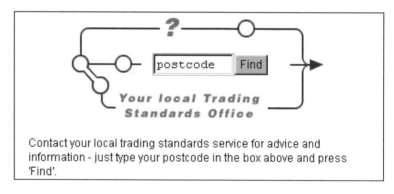

Contact your local trading standards service for advice and information - just type your postcode in the box above and press 'Find'.

## More Internet Handbooks to help you

*Personal Finance on the Internet*, Graham Jones (Internet Handbooks)
*Using Credit Cards on the Internet*, Graham Jones (Internet Handbooks)
*Your Privacy on the Internet*, Kye Valongo (Internet Handbooks)

http://www.internet-handbooks.co.uk

# 2 Searching for information

**In this chapter we will explore:**

▶ *searching the internet*
▶ *internet search engines and directories*
▶ *search utilities*
▶ *shopping portal sites*

## Searching the internet

Finding your way around the internet can seem very confusing to begin with, but the basic method is actually quite easy. Shops and stores are found in one major part of the internet, the world wide web, which consists of hundreds of millions of web pages.

The usual way to look up something on the web is to go to the web site of a well-known search engine or internet directory. You then type in some key words into the little search box provided, and within a few seconds your screen will display a list of web pages containing the information you require. Click on any item in the list, and you will be taken to that particular page. These services are free and open to everyone. There are two main types:

▶ *Search engines* – These are also sometimes known as spiders or crawlers. They have highly sophisticated search tools that automatically seek out web sites across the internet. These trawl through and index literally millions of web pages. As a result they often find information that is not listed in directories.

▶ *Internet directories* – These are developed and compiled by people. Authors submit their web site details and they are assigned to certain areas on the directory. Yahoo! is the biggest and best-known of these.

Most people nowadays refer to directories as search engines and lump the two together. Popular search engines have now become big web sites in their own right, usually combining many useful features. As well as search boxes where you can type key words to summarise what you are looking for, you will usually also find handy directories of information, news, email and many other services. There are hundreds if not thousands of search engines freely available. The biggest and best known include AltaVista, Excite, Infoseek, Lycos and Yahoo! (the most popular of all).

*Bookmarking your favourite web sites*
Your browser (usually Internet Explorer or Netscape Navigator) enables you to save the addresses of any web sites you specially like, and may

# Searching for information. . . . . . . . . . . . . . . . . . . . . . . . . . . . . . . . . . . . . . . . . . . . . . . . .

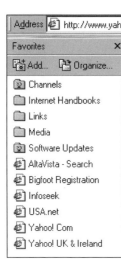

want to revisit. These are called Bookmarks in Netscape, or Favorites in Internet Explorer (US spelling). In either case, while you are viewing the web site, just click on the relevant button on your browser's toolbar – Bookmarks or Favorites as the case may be. This produces a little drop-down menu that you click on to add the site concerned. When you want to revisit that site later, just click again on the same button. Click the name of the web site you bookmarked earlier, and within a few seconds it will open for you.

## Internet search engines and directories

*AltaVista*

http://www.altavista.com

http://www.altavista.co.uk/

AltaVista is one of the most popular search sites among web users world wide. It contains details of millions of web pages on its massive and ever-growing database. You can either follow the trails of links from its home page, or (better) type in your own key words into its search box. You can even search in about 25 different languages.

Fig. 12. The popular internet directory and search engine AltaVista has an enormous number of worldwide shopping links.

*Ask Jeeves*

http://www.askjeeves.com/

Ask Jeeves offers a slightly different approach to searches. It invites you to ask questions on the internet just as you would of a friend or colleague. For example you could type in something like: 'Where can I find out about Italian food?' Jeeves retrieves the information, drawing from a knowledge base of millions of standard answers.

*Deja*
http://www.deja.com/
Deja was founded in 1995 as the first web site exclusively dedicated to searching and archiving Usenet newsgroups. With more than six million page views per day, it has established itself as the leading purveyor of online discussion, offering access to over 45,000 newsgroups and other discussion forums such as internet chat and internet mailing lists.

*Excite*
http://www.excite.com
http://www.excite.co.uk/
Excite is another of the top ten search engines and directories on the internet. To refine your search, simply click the check boxes next to the words you want to add and then click the Search Again button. There are separate Excite home pages for several different countries and cultures including Australia, China, France, Germany, Italy, Japan, Netherlands, Spain, Sweden, and the USA.

*Global Online Directory*
http://www.god.co.uk/
Launched in 1996, GOD is fairly unusual among search engines in that it is UK-based, and aims to be a premier European search service. Features of the site include a 'global search' for web sites by country, state, province, county or even city by city, narrowing down the information for a more focused result.

*Google*
http://www.google.com
This is a new and innovative search site. It matches your query to the text in its index, to find relevant pages. For instance, it looks at what the pages linking to that page have to say about it, so the rating partly depends on outside opinions.

*HotBot*
http://hotbot.lycos.com/
This is an impressive, very popular, and well-classified search engine and directory, once independent but now part of the rapidly growing Lycos empire (see below).

*Infoseek (Go Network)*
http://infoseek.go.com/
In 1994, the American netpreneur Steve Kirsch founded Infoseek with the aim of helping people unleash the power of the internet. He pioneered a suite of powerful, high-quality and easy-to-use search tools. Infoseek is one of the leading search engines on the internet, and is now part of the Go entertainment network.

*Internet Address Finder*
http://www.iaf.net/
The IAF is used by millions of web users for searching and finding the

# Searching for information............................................

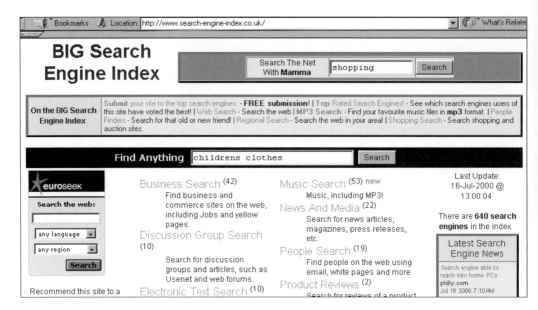

**BIG Search Engine Index**

Search The Net With **Mamma**    `shopping`    [Search]

**On the BIG Search Engine Index**

Submit your site to the top search engines. · **FREE submission!** | Top Rated Search Engines! · See which search engines users of this site have voted the best! | Web Search · Search the web | **MP3 Search** · Find your favourite music files in **mp3** format. | People Finders · Search for that old or new friend! | Regional Search · Search the web in your area! | Shopping Search · Search shopping and auction sites.

**Find Anything** `childrens clothes` [Search]

euroseek

**Search the web:**

any language
any region
[Search]

Recommend this site to a

Business Search (42)
Find business and commerce sites on the web, including Jobs and yellow pages.

Discussion Group Search (10)
Search for discussion groups and articles, such as Usenet and web forums.

Electronic Text Search (10)

Music Search (53) new
Music, including MP3!

News And Media (22)
Search for news articles, magazines, press releases, etc.

People Search (19)
Find people on the web using email, white pages and more

Product Reviews (2)
Search for reviews of a product

Last Update:
16-Jul-2000 @
13:00:04

There are **640 search engines** in the index.

Latest Search Engine News
Search engine able to reach into home PCs
philly.com
Jul 16 2000 7:10AM

Fig. 13. The UK web site Big Search Engine Index is an excellent place to find all kinds of specialist search engines if you are looking for something very specific.

names, email addresses, and now Intel internet videophone contacts, of other users world wide. With millions of addresses it is one of the most comprehensive email directories on the internet. By registering, you could enable others to get in touch with you.

*Internet Public Library*
http://www.ipl.org/ref/
The 'Ask-a-Question' service at the Internet Public Library is experimental. The librarians who work here are mostly volunteers with other full-time librarian jobs. Your question is received at the IPL Reference Centre and the mail is reviewed once a day and questions are forwarded to a place where all the librarians can see them and answer them. Replies are sent as soon as possible, advising whether your question has been accepted or rejected. If it has been accepted, you should receive an answer to in two to seven days.

*List of Search Engines – Big Search Engine Index*
http://www.search-engine-index.co.uk/
This enterprising British site offers a free list of hundreds of search engines, covering different topics. There are software search engines, multiple search engines, email/news search engines, web search engines, commercial search engines, word reference, science search, law search, TV, film and music search, press search, image search, technology manufacturers search, and localised search engines.

*Liszt*
http://www.liszt.com/
Since the 1970s, people have been joining electronic mailing lists to discuss their favourite topics by email, and to have the latest information and news downloaded to their computer. Basically, a mailing list is a commu-

nity whose subscribers can discuss a certain subject by email. Today, Liszt offers the largest index of mailing lists available on the internet, covering every conceivable area of interest. There are more than 90,000 lists in all. Liszt also offers a Usenet newsgroups directory and an IRC chat directory.

*Lycos*
http://www.lycos.com
http://www.lycos.co.uk
Lycos is another of the top ten worldwide web search engines. Lycos is the name for a type of ground spider. It searches document titles, headings, links, and keywords, and returns the first few words of each page it indexes for your search. Founded in 1995, Lycos was one of the earliest search and navigation sites designed to help people find information more easily and quickly on the world wide web. The core technology was developed at Carnegie Mellon University. Lycos sites have been launched in several different countries.

*Metacrawler*
http://www.metacrawler.com/
MetaCrawler was originally developed by Erik Selberg and Oren Etzioni at the University of Washington, and released to the internet in 1995. In response to each user query, it incorporates results from all the top search engines. It collates the results, eliminates duplication, scores the results, and thus provides the user with a list of relevant sites.

*Metaplus*
http://www.metaplus.com/uk.html
Metaplus is a metalist of the best internet directories, and also offers direct links to some of the most essential sites. This is its UK page, containing hundreds of classifications to explore, from search and news, to business, travel, finance and many more.

*Scoot Yahoo!*
http://scoot.yahoo.co.uk
Yahoo! has combined with the British directory Scoot to offer an excellent search facility for those looking for UK-oriented information, businesses and organisations. Once you have found the organisation you are looking for, you can click straight into their web site if they have one.

*Search.com*
http://www.search.com/
This service is run by CNET, one of the world's leading new-media companies. From the home page you can search yellow pages, phone numbers, email addresses, message boards, software downloads, and easily do all kinds of special searches. The site makes use of more than 700 different search engines. CNET also owns SavvySearch.

# Searching for information..........................................

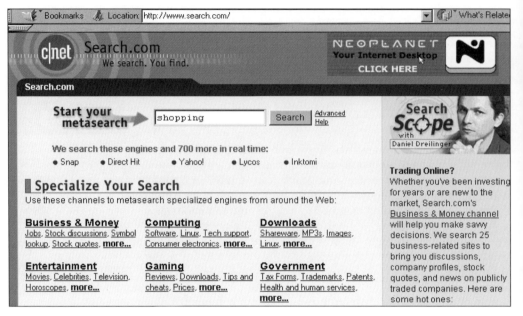

Fig. 14. Search.Com is another powerful internet search engine, capable of retrieving links to millions of pages.

*UK Directory*

http://www.ukdirectory.co.uk/

Somewhat slow to load, this is a useful directory listing of a large number of UK-based web sites. You can browse it or search it. Well-classified by subject matter, it is simple and intuitive to use. You don't need to know the name of the company, service or person to find what you want. Just look in the category that best suits your needs. It is as easy to use as a telephone directory.

*UK Index*

http://www.ukindex.co.uk/

This is another directory of sites in or about the UK. It assigns sites to broad categories to help you with searching. The depth of information seems variable. A search for Shops produced 199 results, but one for Video produced 475.

*UK Plus*

http://www.ukplus.co.uk/

This search engine and database belongs to the group which owns the *Daily Mail, London Evening Standard* and various regional newspapers. It has built a large store of web site reviews written by a team of experienced journalists. Although it concentrates on UK web sites, you will also find many from all over the world.

*Webcrawler*

http://webcrawler.com/

Webcrawler is a fast worker and returns an impressive list of links. It analyses the full text of documents, allowing the searcher to locate key words which may have been buried deep within a document's text. Webcrawler is now part of Excite.

*World Email Directory*
http://www.worldemail.com/
This site is dedicated to email, finding people and locating businesses and organisations. WED has access to an estimated 18 million email addresses and more than 140 million business and phone addresses world wide. Here you'll find everything from email software, to email list servers, many world wide email databases, business, telephone and fax directories and a powerful email search engine.

*Yahoo!*
http://www.yahoo.com
http://www.yahoo.co.uk
Yahoo! was the first substantial internet directory, and is still one of the best for free general searching. It contains millions of links categorised by subject. From one of its home pages (as above) you can 'drill down' through the categories to find what you want, or carry out your own searches using keywords. The service also offers world news, sport, weather, email, chat, retailing facilities, clubs and many other features. Yahoo! is probably one of the search engines and directories you will use time after time.

## Search utilities

*WebFerret*
http://www.ferretsoft.com
WebFerret is an excellent functional search utility. You can type in your query offline, and when you connect it searches the web until it has collected all the references you have specified – up to 9,999 if you wish.

Fig. 15. WebFerret is a very handy search utility, which trawls through several of the big search engines simultaneously. Here it is being used to search for camcorders.

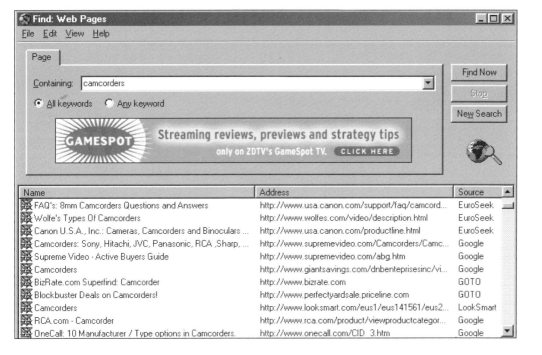

33

WebFerret queries several of the well-known search engines at the same time, and discards duplicate results. It queries include AltaVista, Yahoo!, Infoseek, Excite, and several others. You can immediately visit the URLs it finds, even while WebFerret is still running. The program is free, and simplicity itself. It only takes a few minutes to download from FerretSoft. Highly recommended.

### Shopping portal sites

*Antiques Directory*
http://www.antiques-directory.co.uk/
The directory brings together 17,000 UK antique dealers, antique centres, architectural antiques, collectables dealers, rare book dealers, coin and metal dealers, antique restorers, antique and art valuers, art galleries, fine art dealers, auctioneers and an antique fairs diary. A clickable map of the UK on the home page enables you to identify dealers in a particular area.

*BigYellow*
http://www.bigyellow.com/
This is a massive online USA yellow pages directory, which includes a vast number of shopping and information links.

*Britishmailorder*
http://www.britishmailorder.com/
Rather basic in appearance, this web site nevertheless contains a large number of links to suppliers and catalogues of all kinds of British goods. Click on the mail order category of your choice and see what the listed companies have to offer, everything from audio and autos to videos and wine.

Fig. 16.
Britishmailorder.com site specialises in making British goods available worldwide, for example to anglophiles and expatriates.

*Buyer's Index*
http://www.buyersindex.com/
Buyer's Index is a search engine for anyone wanting to buy, whether on-line or offline. You can search 17,000 web shopping sites and North American mail order catalogues containing more than 96 million products for individuals and businesses.

*Classic England Shopping Mall*
http://www.classicengland.co.uk/
This one offers everything from bacon cured the traditional way to skin care products. If you are baffled for gift ideas or for latest additions to the site you can check out the What's New section. Categories include: antiques, chocolates and candies, clothing and jewellery, collectibles, classic recipes, gifts, health and beauty, home and gardens, hotels and dining. Click a category to see a list of online shops with a short description of what the shop offers. Search is by drop-down list. The site includes a currency converter.

*Compuserve Shopping Centre*
http://www.compuserve.co.uk/shoppingcentre/
The site is divided into three floors, which can be a little confusing as there is no site map saying what is found on each floor, forcing the shopper to go through all the floors to find what they are looking for. On each one a list of shops is featured.

*Cybermall*
http://www.cybermall.com
Cybermall claims to have 'evaluated hundreds of online malls and selected only the very best sites'. There is a brief description of the various malls and stores. This is a huge packed site, but despite its size, well organised and clearly laid out – definitely one to bookmark.

*Electronic Yellow Pages*
http://www.eyp.co.uk
Before the internet, when looking for a competitive quote for something, what did you do? Most people simply turned to Yellow Pages and started phoning around. In a more sophisticated way you can do the same kind of thing online. These electronic yellow pages are organised on the same lines as the paper edition. Just type in the details of the information you need – anything from bathroom equipment to wines and spirits – and it quickly searches for such services in your local area. Unfortunately not all searches tell you whether the company you are looking for has a web page.

*Excite Shopping*
http://www.excite.com/shopping/
If you sign up with Excite you will receive special online benefits such as personalised savings from your favourite brands and stores, targeted to your particular shopping interests, digital coupons you can redeem online and printable coupons that can be printed from your computer. You will

have your own personalised online account for when you are ready to shop. While you are signing up, take a look at Excite's weekly top five offers. If finances are tight, click the free stuff category and check out what Excite has on offer. Excite also offers online auctions and classified ads. This is a clearly organised, bright and cheerful site – definitely worth a look.

*Funsites*
http://www.funsites.com/sh-malls.html
The site is not the easiest to read, with small white lettering on a brown/black background, and it can take a while to download. However, it does open up a host of shopping malls (mostly American), each with numerous retailers. You can find malls, catalogues, department and chain stores and other goods and services offering products related to arts and entertainment, autos, fashion, food, gifts, health and fitness, household, professional services, sports, recreation, technology and travel.

*High Street Central*
http://www.highstreetcentral.com
High Street Central is a web and book directory covering a wide range of subjects with links to millions of sites and categorised books. There is an unusual search facility here: press Control + F which brings up the search engine. The site organisation is rather unusual, too. Half of it is devoted to web sites and the other half to books. The two headings tend to overlap so this might be a bit confusing. There is certain amount of sponsorship to get through before you reach the category you are looking for.

---

**\*NEW\* - i-Stores**
Got anything to se
Part of the eBi

iStores Departments

»**Auctions**
eBid

»**Books & Magazines**
Computer Manuals

»**Cars & Transport**
your site here

»**Clothes & Fashion**
your site here

»**Computers**
your site here

»**Dept Stores & Malls**

---

*I-Stores*
http://www.i-stores.co.uk/
I-Stores is a directory of UK-based secure online stores. It includes auctions, games and toys, books and magazines, groceries, computer manuals, cars and transport, health and lifestyle, clothes and fashion, hobbies and crafts, computers, home and garden, department stores and malls, electrical goods, entertainment, travel and holidays, and flowers and gifts.

*Internetics*
http://www.internetics.co.uk/shop/
Internetics is a very useful guide to online secure UK stores, and has assembled links to over 300 stores to choose from. There is a database search facility to help you decide where to look. Shops are divided into categories such as books, computers and software, food and wine and games. All are marked with the number of sites each category contains. The site is updated daily and shows which new sites have been added. Or, you can go with the tried and tested top 30 favourite sites. If you like the site, you might want to subscribe to its email newsletter.

*Irish Shopping Centres*
http://www.angelfire.com/hi/shoppingcentres
This is a guide to 'real world' shopping centres in Ireland. The ones listed

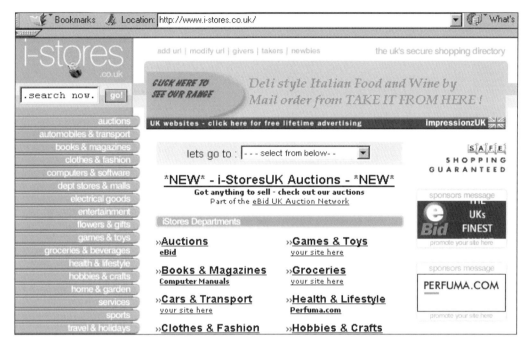

are Harbour Place Shopping Centre in Mullingar, Bridge Centre in Tullamore, Golden Island Shopping Centre in Athlone, Erneside Centre in Enniskillen, Sligo Shopping Cenre and the Courtyard in Letterkenny. Altogether about 170 stores are represented. Only a few of them are as yet hyperlinked.

*Link of Malls*
http://www.bltg.com/malllist/
This is a Canadian-based site. It provides a useful guide to mainly Canadian and American internet shopping malls and a short description of what each site offers. For example, Net Avenue offers a sizeable music and book store, and there is a very unusual Maori gift site for those interested in the native culture of New Zealand.

*Lycos Shop*
http://shop.lycos.com/
This is a major global shopping portal site developed by the search engine, Lycos. There is a search box at the top of the home page where you can type in what you are looking for. Among the categories are auctions, automotive, books, clothing, computer hardware, communication services, consumer electronics, department stores and malls, flowers and gifts, travel and food and wine. Other resources offered are books, classified, homes and loans, music, new and used cars and domain registration. You could shop with a Lycos MasterCard.

*Malls Metalist*
http://malls.com/metalist.html
This is a substantial resource, leading to hundreds if not thousands of

# Searching for information.............................................

Fig.18. Malls.com is one of many similar American web sites dedicated to worldwide shopping. There is a vast number of shopping links to be found here.

shopping malls all over the internet. It links to large malls, cyber villages, cyber cities, global malls, ethnic and country malls, theme malls, regional, city and street malls. The shops in the shopping channel carry a brief description of the goods they offer. There are video games, a chat room with rules for chatting, a page of jokes, a page for classified ads, and many other features. Each day includes some new bargain offers.

*Lifestyle*
http://www.lifestyle.co.uk/
This site is meant to lets you shop according to your lifestyle. Check out the New Section which tells you all about the latest additions to the site. The Friends section is not a lonely hearts site, so go there if you are look-ing for business, not personal, contacts. There are some rather unusual sites to see; for example, in transport an Identified Flying Objects site caters for all your aviation needs. One area is called Women on the Net. There is quite a lot of content devoted to sports, and if you need a break, the Weird and Wacky site may give you just the lift you need.

*Outlets Online*
http://www.outletsonline.com/shopndx.html
The site lists outlet centres in the USA, Canada and internationally. You must register first, which takes about 24 hours to be confirmed. The site uses a secure transaction facility that protects your privacy. As a regis-tered guest you will receive occasional emails regarding outlet events and retailer sales taking place at your nearest outlet centres and retail stores. The search facility, which is on a separate page from the home page, gives you access to the contents of all the publicly available web documents on OutletsOnline.

*Portobello*
http://www.portobello.co.uk/
Yes, here is the world's largest antiques market now online. Click this site to stroll around London's Portobello Road and get an idea of where you might find a real treasure. The site offers lots of information about the market such as opening times and where to eat. A bonus is that the site appears in five foreign languages – useful for visitors who want to plan their visit before leaving home. There is a handy map to print out to help you find your way around. But before you leave, click the drop-down menu to get an idea of the goods and services on offer.

*Retail Co UK*
http://www.retail.co.uk
This is an unusual site in stylish black and white. You access the list of UK high street stores and suppliers using a drop-down list. A blue dot next to a shop means that it supports online transactions. Each site is followed by a short paragraph describing the goods on offer. It seems to be geared toward the more upmarket shopper. The selection of sites is fairly limited and carries the usual selection of books, computers, fashion and gifts, though it does offer some sites that do not appear in the usual shopping sites, e.g. Jaguar, Oddbins, and Nissan.

*Robins FYI*
http://www.robinsfyi.com
This enterprising site lists over 200 online malls in alphabetical order. There are around 600 pages, including some 1,600 files and over 6,000 external links. If you find it confusing, go to the site map, which displays the different features. You might want to visit the section on animals (which contains a whole sub-section with appropriate links on every-thing from cats to snakes) or holidays (check out the Christmas horror stories). FYI is a cross between a personal page, a directory site and a web guide. The listed sites are inspected by the webmaster.

*Shop.Co*
http://www.shop.co.uk/home.htm
There is a very long home page but no search engine for finding specific sites. Select what you are looking for from the categories. Once you have entered all your criteria, the site will display a list of those businesses which match your requirements. The categories include animals and pets, bathrooms and bathroom goods, carpets and catering. Clicking one of these opens a page of sub-categories, which leads to a list of hyperlinked shops. A brief description of the shops would be useful. However, URLs are included with the hyperlinks. The site has yellow let-tering on a black background, which is not very easy to read. The site downloads quickly as it is virtually graphics-free.

*Shop Guide*
http://www.shopguide.com/
Shop Guide is a shopping guide and search engine for over 20,000 of online stores, virtual malls and cyber shops, complete with reviews and

shopguide.com

FREE Merchant Listing
NEW
Advertisers
Frequent Shoppers
Certified Medallion
U.S. Local ShopGuide
International ShopGui
Company Profile
Contact Us
Internet Source Book
ShopGuideNews

ratings. There are over 450 secure UK shops in the shopping directory. There are plenty of incentives, freebies and coupons for bargain shoppers. It covers clothing and accessories, gifts, holidays, entertainment, auto and travel, health and beauty, books, music, video, home and garden, business-to-business, household goods, computer technology, office supplies, department stores, mail order, sports and leisure, electronics, appliances, toys and children, food and drink, and more. If you sign up for the free email newsletter you might win a flight to New York.

**Auction** (67)
everything and anything...

**Business to Business**
connecting to business serv

**Cars & Motorcycles** (4
dealers, parts, accessories..

**Computer Services** (6
ISPs, technical help, graph

**Electronics** (374)
cameras, MP3s, appliances

**Fashion & Apparel** (37
women's, sportswear, suits,

**Flowers & Gifts** (4259)
florists, gift baskets, collecti

**General Services** (194
legal, personal, weddings..

**Hobbies** (839)
crafts, collecting, special in

*ShopNow*
http://www.shopnow.com
ShopNow is one of the leading shopping networks and directories on the internet. It links to more than 60,000 merchants offering millions of products. It has over 7,000 affiliate sites, and was named the number one online shopping mall for the first four months of 2000. ShopNow is a division of Network Commerce Inc, whose other services include the shopping comparison agent Bottom Dollar.

*Shopping Centres*
http://www.shopping-centres.com/
The site opens with photographs of four shopping centres. Click the appropriate photograph to enter the site which takes you to a map of the UK. In the upper left-hand corner are links to an A to Z of centres, latest news, factory outlets, and about our service. The A to Z leads to a list of hyperlinked shopping centres, and the names of towns they are in.

*Shop the Malls*
http://www.shop-the-malls.htm
The search engine is a drop-down list which contains the site's categories. These are divided into merchants, malls and online shops, and cover food, fragrances, gardening, health and beauty and finance. Each category contains a list of participating shops. Confusingly, the page format changes for each category. Among the features are a chat room, cartoons, news, and a Single's Hotspot.

*Shoppers Universe*
http://shoppersuniverse.co.uk/
This shopping mall offers global delivery, secure transactions and fast downloading graphics. It says: 'The stores are dedicated to bringing you all the top brand names you'd expect to find in the high street shops.' Selections include everything from lingerie and clothing to sports and electrical equipment. Click the category on the left to reveal the participating shops. Shoppers Universe employs a sophisticated multi-level payment validation procedure which includes the automatic encryption of payment details.

*Shopping Center Net*
http://www.shoppingcenter.net/
The sites here are split into categories and subcategories: animals (pets, wildlife), arts (hobbies, craft supplies), books (books, magazines), com-

puters (hardware, software), gifts (flowers, baskets, novelties) and so on. Each site has a brief description of the goods or services available. Most are hyperlinked. There is a search engine showing the number of matches. There are some free services, for example handy reminders so you never forget important anniversaries, greeting cards, and classifieds where you can place an ad.

*Shopping Malls Directory*
http://www.shoppingmallsdirectory.com/malls.htm
This starts with a very long home page that lists all the malls in alphabetical order but for some reason start with the letter T.

*Shopping Villages UK*
http://www.shoppingvillages.co.uk/
This is a very useful and comprehensive online directory of UK shopping villages, outlet stores, and factory shops. They say: 'This must be one of Britain's best kept secrets, a collection of shops that sell top quality brand named products vastly discounted from 30 per cent to 80 per cent off normal prices.' You can submit a request to be kept up to date about the site.

*Shops on the Net*
http://www.shopsonthenet.com
The sites here are listed by categories such as alcohol and tobacco products, accessories, auctions, music and videos. Under each one is a list of sub-topics. You click the desired category to see a list of entries. Entries include the country of origin, the URL, Trustmark (if appropriate) and a brief description of the shop. You can also see how many entries there are per category. There is a search engine at the top of the page. The site has some useful product comparisons, side-by-side charts, product reviews, discussion groups, classifieds and shopping links and a merchants rating system. Check out the Hot Offers page for free and discount offers.

*Shop Yell*
http://www.shopyell.co.uk
This site is related to the Yellow Pages. Select a category (books, film and music, clothing and accessories, computer and office, computer software, food and drink, and games, hobbies and toys) and click for more information. This takes you to a store listing where you must click again to access the store's site. The search engine enables you to search by business type or company name and location. The web search is limited to the UK. Confusingly, the web search can also be done from a different list of categories than those presented on the home page. You can also search by business type, access a five-day weather forecast, and find information on your local neighbourhood.

*Stores A-Z*
http://www.storesa-z.com/
This is a directory of around 1,500 well-known American chain stores, as well as catalogue and mail order companies, internet retailers, and more.

# Searching for information..........................................

**Gifts & Gadgets**

**Shopping from Yell**

For an individual description of each store simply move your cursor over the shop name

**our shops**
⊕ = new shop

▸ Alternative Gift Company
n Belgian Chocolates Direct
▸ Index
n Lands' End
▸ Online Records
n Select Marketing Ltd
▸ Shoppingcentre.net
n StuckForAGift.com
▸ The Best of British
n The Big Watch Co.
▸ Thorntons
n Web Electricals

The stores listed offer a variety of products and services that can be purchased securely online.

Each of our stores uses a completely safe and secure encryption system to take your credit card information.

For On-line
Quotations
& Cover

want to sell your products ?
➔ suggestion box

⊕ main index

FAQs | Customer Services | Shopping Guide | Feedback | Yell

Fig.19. Don't forget yellow pages. ShopYell is an online version of the traditional version. There are various main categories to explore, such as Gifts & Gadgets illustrated here.

*UK Shopping City*
http://www.ukshops.co.uk/
This is not so much an online shopping centre as a collection of home pages for various UK businesses. You can view the City's tenants in alphabetical order, and see a brief description of each business and its key features. For example, use the search engine to find the Alton Towers page and see what is happening at this popular entertainment park, or take a look at the Argos site to do some catalogue shopping online. There are facilities for seeing what is new in Europe and a Yahoo!-style European Directory of information about Europe.

*UK Yellow Web Directory*
http://www.yell.co.uk/
The yellow pages division of British Telecom operates this site. It is indexed 'by humans' and is searchable. A number of non-UK sites are included in the database. Companies whose names begin with 'The' are listed under T. A Business Compass lists what it considers the best business internet resources, together with links and brief descriptions.

*Which?*
http://www.which.net/
Which? Online has a useful site map of the contents. Click on any of the words here to jump to the starting page of that section. Information in the free area can be seen by anyone with internet access. Information in the members-only area, usually indicated by a red roundel next to the link, is protected. You'll need a username and password to gain access (a free 30-day trial is available). Click the various parts of the site map to access information on managing your money, deciding which car to buy or for

advice on choosing the best holiday package. You can even use Which? as your internet service provider.

*World Shopping Mall and Directory*
http://www.worldshopping.com/
There is plenty of variety here. You could even get paid to surf the web. If you are in spending mode, there is plenty to choose from: arts, antiques, home and garden, specialty shops, sporting goods, tobacco and travel sites. Or how about a free 90-day subscription to your favourite magazine?

*Yahoo! Shop Guide*
http://shopguide.yahoo.com/
If it's online, it should be here. The top internet search directory, Yahoo! has in the last year or so developed its own big shopping centre offering everything from computers to children's clothing. It contains more than 5,000 merchant sites, where you can shop using a special online wallet arrangement. There are classified ads for everything from jobs to flat shares, yellow pages for local services in your area, store listings by category (leisure, food and drink etc), a Yahoo! Visa card, and an online membership program which rewards you for shopping at specific sites. The site naturally has an efficient search engine.

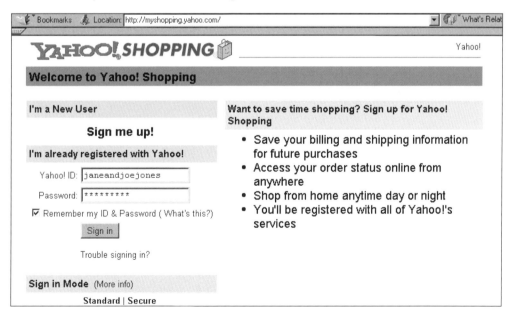

Visit the free Internet HelpZone at
**www.internet-handbooks.co.uk**
Helping you master the internet

# 3 Comparison shopping

### Comparison shopping agents or bots

An interesting phenomenon of internet shopping has been the emergence of 'comparison shopping agents' as a powerful tool for the consumer. Shopping agents are sometimes called bots. Bot is short for robot, and describes a software program given a specific task on a network or on the internet. Bots carry out all kinds of ingenious tasks on the internet, such as searching for information, monitoring sites and alerting people when those sites have changed.

Shopping bots are becoming a key part of the online world. A shopping bot will search the web for the products you specify, and display on your screen a list of merchants with the best deals. The bot will display all the key things you need to know - product name, price and method of payment, availability, speed of service, and shipment. You can then make your order. This greatly reduces the time you might otherwise spend with search engines, and can introduce you to some excellent online stores you would not otherwise have come across. One of the earliest of these shopping agents was Acses. This was targeted at the enormous market for online book sales, pioneered by Amazon and imitated by many competitors.

Comparison shopping makes life very challenging for every online retailer, who has to compete more fiercely than ever before. In early 2000, the world's biggest online auction web site, eBay, used legal action to try and prevent shopping bots harvesting information from its auction rooms.

According to research by US company Jupiter Communications, 77 per cent of buyers have something specific in mind, and 7 per cent of those view several sites before making a purchase. Working with shopping bots will be vital for retailers wanting to survive the online world. Jupiter says that 'Online merchants must create unique shopping experiences and implement loyalty programmes to differentiate themselves from the competition and to convert a portion of these one-time bot-driven shoppers into a loyal customer base.'

### Some top comparison shopping sites

Keep in mind that these shopping bots are just helpers. In the end, the transaction takes still place between you and an online store. Be careful when you are placing your order, especially with an overseas supplier. It is not bound by your local country's consumer protection laws. The best advice is: buyer beware!

Fig. 20. Active Buyer's Guide is one of several price comparison search engines that can do a lot of the hard work for you.

Fig. 21. Buyer's Index is another price comparison agent, which can find you the best deal from among a staggering 150 million product offerings.

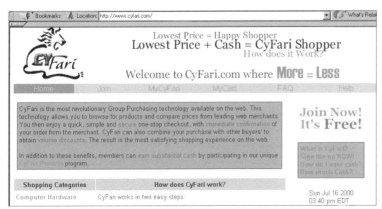

Fig. 22. CyFari is another shopping agent keen to offer its services to you for free.

# Comparison shopping ....................................................

*Active Buyers Guide*
http://www.activebuyersguide.com/
AGG recommends products and merchants according to your requests. It also powers some of the big web shopping portals such as Lycos, Infoseek (GoNetwork), MySimon and DealTime. It is based on something called 'adaptive recommendation technology', which simulates the trade-offs each consumer makes when making shopping decisions.

*All Book Stores*
http://www.allbookstores.com/
This site compares prices on books at 30 online bookstores. You then can click on a link to buy the book from the store you choose. Though the home page takes a while to load, it works at an impressive speed, and provides a total price, including shipping.

*Auction Octopus*
http://www.auctionoctopus.com/
Here's something for everyone with online bid-fever, a multi-auction search engine that provides real-time access to some of the internet's best known auction sites. It queries the sites, receives and interprets each site's results and displays the total results in a convenient listing. For more auction bots, see chapter 4.

**Shopping Categories**
**COMPUTER HARDWARE**
Hardware: *Desktops, Laptop*
*PDAs, etc.*

**ELECTRONICS**
Home Electronics: *TVs, Stere*
*Players,*
*Digital Cameras*

**FUN & GAMES**
Toys: *Pokemon, Board Games*
Sporting Goods, Video Gam

**FOR THE OFFICE**
Office Products: *Binders, Co*
*Pens*

**GIFTS**
Gift Items: *Gift Baskets*

*Bottom Dollar*
http://www.bottomdollar.com/
Consumers can choose between eight product categories, enter a brand name or item, and click on the Go button. Bottom Dollar's shopping bot works in the background to simultaneously query many online retailers and in about ten seconds returns a list of retail outlets with the best prices on that product, including links to their order pages. Bottom Dollar has around 1,700 affiliated merchant sites, and generates over six million product searches per month. It is a division of Network Commerce Inc.

*Buyer's Index*
http://www.buyersindex.com/
Buyer's Index is a powerful search engine for buyers. You can search 11,000 web shopping sites and North American mail order catalogues containing more than 93 million product offerings for individuals and businesses.

*CyFari*
http://www.cyfari.com
One of the more recent comparison sites to emerge is CyFari. Only the book and music search engines are functional at the moment, but the company eventually plans to feature eleven search engines, for clothes, computers, software, movies, toys and other products. It works in two easy steps: first you select a product, compare its price from leading web merchants and place your order. Then Cyfari transmits your order and obtains a confirmation in real time over a secure connection. Alternatively, they can hold your order for the time you specify, and combine it

with those of other buyers. Then, you will either pay the lower volume discount price, or, if that did not materialise, the original price. You can compare prices with ease, make purchases without having to enter your personal information each time, and, if you wish, group your order with others in the hope of volume discounts.

*DealTime*
http://www.dealtime.com/
You can shop for almost anything here. DealTime tracks online shopping sites, auctions, classified ads and sales, and notifies you on your desktop as soon as products become available at your indicated price levels. There are opportunities also to become an affiliate or merchant. They say: 'DealTime is a free online comparison-shopping service that locates the web sites offering deals on the products you want to buy. We don't sell, we list the online merchants, auctions, classifieds and group buying sites that match your shopping criteria. You decide where to shop – no more aimless searching for the hottest online deals. Want to hold out for a better deal? No problem, DealTime remembers what you're looking for and continues searching the web for the latest deals, transmitting your updates instantly via email.'

*Excite Shopping Channel*
http://shopping.excite.com/
The Excite Shopping Channel offers shopping search, departments, resources, and chat and message boards. This is a comprehensive site offering numerous shopping bots and intelligent agents. On the home page click My Alerts. Excite shopping alerts will notify you of new pro-

Fig. 23. Many of the big search engines have now set up their own shopping sites and free price-comparison agents, such as Excite, illustrated here.

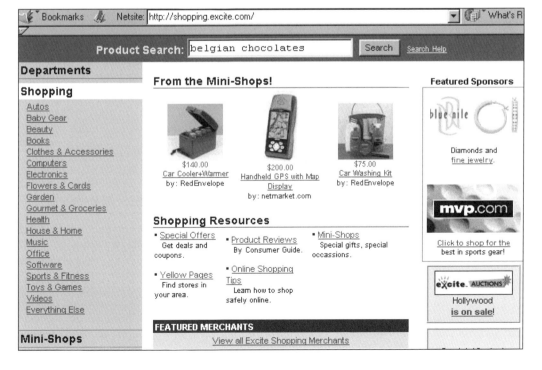

ducts and price changes that match your search criteria. Get alerts delivered by email or on your Excite start page. You must be an Excite member to view or set up alerts.

*Get Hit*
http://www.gethit.com
GetHit offers access to hundreds of ecommerce sites, from top names like Barnes and Noble to obscure niche market companies. There are product categories covering music, books, food, art and pets. There is a handy list of all the vendors in each category. You can quickly see how many have made their prices available, what kind of store they are, and check out their services such as overnight delivery, secure transactions and helplines. Shopping here is versatile. You can hyperlink direct to a store, or search for a product by category. To shop for a product, you enter the name in the Product field at the top of each page, choose a category and click Go. Gethit then displays a list of the sites with the product you want, and the price for the product at that site.

See the iChoose alert work for you!

*iChoose Savings Alert*
http://www.ichoose.com/
The iChoose savings alert is free software that gives you access to better deals on the things you want to buy - books, music, movies, toys, hardware and software, consumer electronics, pet supplies, and more. You can download the software from here. The savings alert instantly delivers better deals to you when you are ready to buy, and pops up with a better deal (if one exists). Founded in April 1999, iChoose is based in Texas.

*myBuyTrek*
http://www.mybuytrek.com/
myBuyTrek is another computer shopper that enables you to research and go online shopping for your favourite products and services. It covers auctions, too. The database seems pretty big. For example, a search for products relating to athletics (running and track sports) turned up more than 1,500 links.

*My Simon*
http://www.mysimon.com/
My Simon is an 'intelligent' comparison shopping agent. Using VLA (virtual learning agent) technology, Simon imitates human navigational behaviour and can be 'taught' to shop at 2,000 merchants in hundreds of product categories on the web. Simon shops in real time, so he will find the right products, at the right place, at the best price. To activate it, just do a keyword search for clothes, books or media products, computers, electronics flowers gourmet, health, home and leisure products, office equipment and supplies, sports goods and toys. The site includes various consumer resources and tools, a newsletter, and a talk area.

*NetBuyer*
http://www.zdnet.com/netbuyer/
NetBuyer is a service of the popular ZDNet computer and internet infor-

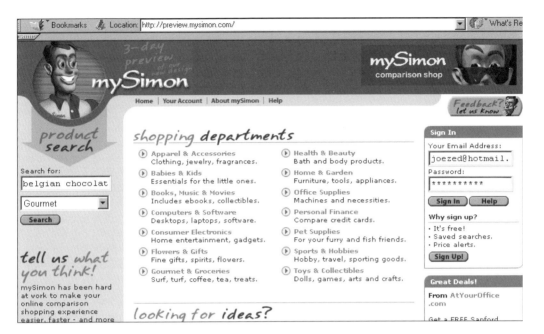

mation web site. It enables you to shop using a full text search or complete category list. It looks impressively comprehensive. There is also some free Windows software called MyZDNet Alerts that you can use to deliver product information directly to your PC. It updates itself during the day over your internet connection. You can download it free from here. When the installation is complete, the alerts window will open and a small icon will appear in your taskbar.

Fig. 24. MySimon is another shopping agent service for the busy online shopper in search of the best deal. The home page is organised by product category, but you can do your own particular search as well.

*NetMarket*
http://www.netmarket.com
NetMarket can save you money on just about anything you want. With a database of some 800,000 branded products at wholesale prices, it offers one of the best selections available. NetMarket uses some of the latest encryption technology, digital certificates, secure commerce servers, and authentication to make sure your personal details are secure online. If your credit card number is stolen online while using Netmarket, and fraudulent charges are made to that credit card, Netmarket say they will reimburse you for the amount not covered by your credit card issuer up to the legal limit.

*PriceScan*
http://www.pricescan.com
PriceScan compares product prices between various online stores. It covers books, computer products, electronics, movies, music, office equipment, sporting goods and video games. It lists vendor prices in its database free of charge. It also obtains product and pricing information from catalogues and magazine ads. It updates its database each day, so that the price you find should be the price you'll pay. Depending on the product you want, you can search by general categories or by specific

criteria. For example, if you want to buy a book you can search by author, title or ISBN. To buy a computer game, you can search by category, platform, manufacturer or licence type. Once you've selected a product, clicking Get Prices displays a list of all the vendors selling that product, and their prices.

*RoboShopper*
http://www.roboshopper.com/
Introduced in 1997, RoboShopper was one of the first internet comparison shopping systems. During the past three years, it has attracted millions of users while earning awards from *USA Today* and ZDNet, where it was a five-star editor's choice. RoboShopper makes online shopping fast and easy. Just tell it what kind of thing are looking for and it will automatically query online stores, displaying the results in a convenient report in your browser window. You can then easily make comparisons and make the best buying decision. Its home page is not the quickest to download. RoboShopper does not store any secure information, such as credit card numbers, on its own system.

*Shopbest*
http://www.shopbest.com/
Shopbest is a British internet shopping service provider established in 1997. It launched its own comparison shopping engine in 1998.

*ShopFind*
http://www.shopfind.com
ShopFind is a web page of Yahoo! Shopping. It give you access to a vast number of Yahoo!-affiliated stores. A search for 'palm pilot', for example, yielded a list of 615 products in 95 different stores. A convenient feature of this service is that you can click to view the products list sorted by

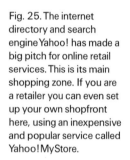

Fig. 25. The internet directory and search engine Yahoo! has made a big pitch for online retail services. This is its main shopping zone. If you are a retailer you can even set up your own shopfront here, using an inexpensive and popular service called Yahoo! MyStore.

price range. Click on the one you want, and you will arrive at a shopping cart to complete your order.

*Shopping Explorer*
http://www.shoppingexplorer.com
Shopping Explorer is a software program that helps you to shop on the internet. You can download it from here. It is quite easy to use. Just tell Shopping Explorer what you are looking for and it will search the web sites of hundreds of online merchants all over the world on your behalf. New shops are constantly becoming available. During a search, Shopping Explorer will automatically detect if your current list of merchants needs updating. If necessary, you will be given the option to download the new merchant sites and install them automatically.

*SmartBots.Com*
http://www.smartbots.com/
This is a very useful directory of price shopping robots on the internet. It provides information (not always up to date) about a variety of shopping bots to help you automatically find the lowest prices on products by searching dozens of online stores for the best prices.

*SmartShop*
http://www.smartshop.com/
If you are worried about the 'extras', for example if buying from an overseas supplier, this could be the site for you. It not only compares prices, but takes into account shipping costs and special promotions. It then suggests which one is the best overall deal.

*TechBargains*
http://www.techbargains.com/
This one focuses on technology-related products. It scours the web and presents the highlights on its home page.

*TechShopper*
http://www.techweb.com/shopper/
TechShopper is a service of CMPNet. It provides a research-and-buy facility that focuses on hardware, software and PCs. The main product groupings are desktop computers, storage, digital cameras, notebook computers, input devices, multimedia hardware, handheld computers, modems, networking hardware, servers, printers, boards and chips, monitors and projectors, scanners and software.

*ValueFind*
http://www.valuefind.com/
This looks to be a comprehensive service. It takes your request and searches for the best deal from retailers, online auction rooms and classified ads. You can limit your search to a specific price range and to certain sites. You can also set up a want list to search on an ongoing basis and let you know when it finds what you want at the right price.

*ValueSpeed*
http://www.valuespeed.com/
ValueSpeed is a little piece of software adds a Compare button to your web browser. It automatically compares prices whenever you click on it. You can download the software from here.

*Web Market*
http://www.webmarket.com
WebMarket searches the top online stores to bring you the best prices on the items you are looking for. Just choose a category to start your search. WebMarket is part of the Go2Net organisation, which also owns the well-known search engines Dogpile and Metacrawler.

*What's the Deal.com*
http://www.whatsthedeal.com/
In addition to links to hundreds of online stores, this one benefits from consumer reviews and expert advice. The main listed categories are auctions, hardware, office products, books, home and garden, software computers, kitchen, sporting goods, electronics, magazines, toys, fragrances, movies, videos and PCs, games, gifts, music, and others. It offers updated links to other price trackers and product review sites, various consumer hotlines and resources, freebies, coupons and 'earn money' sites. Based in Los Angeles, California, the site first appeared in 1999.

Fig. 26. What's The Deal is yet another option for shoppers who just want the best prices without the bother of having to find individual online stores.

## Finding out more

*Bot Spot*
http://www.botspot.com
Bot Spot can tell you all you need to know about all the design and use of
bots and intelligent agents on the net. Its resources include 14 searchable
bot classification databases, FAQs, libraries, articles, newsletters, ejour-
nals, listservs, conferences, conference proceedings, a book store,
commerce bots, shopping bots, knowledge bots, search bots, artificial
intelligence and much more.

# 4 Catalogues, classifieds and auctions

In this chapter we will explore:

▶ *catalogue web sites*
▶ *classified advertising*
▶ *online auctions*

. . . . . . . . . . . . . . . . . . . . . . . . . . . . . . . . . . . . . . . . . . . . . .

## Catalogue web sites

The internet lends itself wonderfully well to catalogue shopping. Indeed, it is traditional mail order shoppers who are leading the way in online shopping. Internet technology means that it is relatively cheap for retailers to publish masses of colour information online, cheaper perhaps that the cost of expensively printed and mailed catalogues. The following sites represent a mixture of traditional and online catalogues, and open the way to a fantastic range of products which are potentially available. In the whole history of shopping, your choice has never been greater.

*Argos*
http://www.argos.co.uk/

Fig. 27. The internet is a great place to find catalogues, both of the electronic and traditional kinds. Catalink is a good place to start your search for free catalogues.

The UK catalogue people offer a range of goods to purchase online. The site is well designed and should appeal to cyber-surfing mums looking to save time and money by shopping online. The site provides guidance, a shopping bag, an order form, online help, store services, store finder and what's new. You can explore DIY, car and garden, sports and leisure, home furnishings, bathroom, bedding, personal care, household, electri-

cal goods, cleaning and utility, kitchen and tableware, sound and vision, telephones and pagers, home office, toys and nursery, clocks, watches and jewellery, and gifts. The graphics are bright and colourful and the lettering big and bold. You can search by key words, catalogue numbers or price range. You can also find details of Argos stores and opening hours.

*Catalink*
http://www.catalink.co.uk/
Catalink is a free UK mail order catalogue resource. You can choose catalogues from a large selection here, arranged under subject headings. When reviewed, the seven most requested catalogues appeared to be the Next Directory, Janet Reger Direct, Freemans, Ocean, Bonsoir, Bravissimo, and Pooh Corner.

*CatalogLink*
http://www.cataloglink.com
The CatalogLink search engine provides you with the catalogues that best match your queries. Searching the site is easy. You can search by catalogue name, by category, by type of product, or by any other parameter that you decide is relevant. The site provides access to literally hundreds of catalogues covering everything from fitness and fashion to food and pet supplies. Most of the catalogues here are free, and will be delivered within three to four weeks. Rather than listing the catalogues themselves, the site lists the companies that offer the catalogues. CatalogLink says it complies with guidelines for collecting consumer information.

BROWSE CATEGORIES

Apparel & Accessories

Beauty, Health & Fitness

Collectibles

Computers, Electronics & Office

Flowers & Gifts

Food & Gourmet

Home & Family

*Catalog Mart*
http://catalog.savvy.com
Using Catalog Mart you can arrange to receive just about any catalogue offered in the US today. The site offers a staggering 10,000 different catalogues in more than 800 topic areas. All of them are free. Select the topic you are interested in and fill out the electronic order form. This form is forwarded to the appropriate companies. The selection is vast: everything from active sportswear to wrought iron furniture. However, the site itself is very small and could be better organised if the topics were arranged in categories, rather than forcing reader to scroll through a long list of categories to see what is on offer.

*The Catalog Site*
http://www.catalogsite.com
This one includes a useful database search and a list of more than 200 catalogues with a short description of what each one offers, including gift certificates. The site helpfully distinguishes between companies that offer catalogues only, and those that also offer online shopping. The site is organised by catalogue index A to Z, a catalogue update, a sales and bargains section, catalogues online, gifts and gift certificates, catalogue reviews, a newsletter, and catalogue gossip. You carry out your search by catalogue name or by category of interest.

## Catalog Savings

http://www.catalogsavings.com

There are three ways to search here: you can click a category, use the catalogue search facility, or use a broad product search facility. The service features new catalogues and savings in the areas of arts, hobbies and crafts, computer and office supplies, fun gadgets, pets, gardening, exercise and sporting goods. If you click the drop-down menu you will see a list of companies offering catalogues, or you can enter a description in the product search box. The site is updated daily and features a different list of featured catalogues. The catalogue profile offers a detailed description of the catalogue as well as a savings certificate offer that you can use when ordering from that particular company.

## Catalog World

http://www.catalogworld.com

Here you can request a print version of a catalogue, or access a merchant's online catalogue. Just choose a category, or search by keywords for the type of product you want (e.g. chocolate) or for a specific merchant. The Catalog World 'community' consists of 18,000 shoppers and 10,000 catalogue merchants. A database search for women's clothing, for example, turned up 564 records. The catalogue included Christmas gifts for children, an online bookshop specialising in mystery novels, and even an international dating service matching foreign women with British men.

## Freemans

http://www.freemans.co.uk

Freemans is an old-established UK catalogue seller. Its search engine enables you to trawl through the entire online catalogue quickly and efficiently. You can be very specific or general (for example, type in the word shirts or blouses). The web site is orientated to ecommerce. Goods can be delivered anywhere in the world, subject to an international delivery charge. To purchase an item, just click the trolley icon and follow the instructions on the page. You must also enter an email address and password, determined on your first visit to the site. The Freemans site is fully secure for online transactions. You might find the animations rather distracting.

## Grattan

http://www.grattan.co.uk

Grattan offers a huge range of fashion, home, and leisure goods.

## Innovations

http://www.innovations.co.uk

The well-known pocket size consumer magazine *Innovations* drops through millions of UK letter boxes each year, featuring the latest in high-tech gadgets and inventions. Hundreds of ingenious products are available through its online catalogue. All online transactions are secure. Choose UK Customer if you already have an existing account, or UK Guest if this is your first visit. The catalogue doesn't contain a description of the product so it can be difficult to estimate the dimensions, sizes, weights, and colours. You can ask for catalogues from other sites, but the choice is limited. The main categories are housewares, garden, personal care, sports and leisure, small and large electrical, gifts and accessories, office and computer, apparel, lighting and textiles.

*Kays*
http://www.kaysnet.com/
Kays is a leading name in the catalogue business. In its online catalogue you will find an extensive range of 25,000 products. It operates a free delivery service within the UK and all transactions are secure. You can shop by department or lifestyle, and departments include ladies wear, lingerie, nursery, children's wear and a toy shop. There are also some lifestyle features – young mum, teenager, trendsetter, and so on. Follow the steps to select your order and then place it into the Internet Shopping Bag. On the downside it is fairly time-consuming to access the site and takes several clicks to get to the desired page. You must first select the object and then click preview. The pictures are rather small and hard to see.

*Nanana*
http://www.nanana.com/catalogs.html
Nanana is an excellent base to look for a large number of free shopping catalogues from different suppliers. The catalogues deal with clothes, fashion, outdoor gear, electronics, gifts, wedding, women's goods, games, computers, pets, hobbies, art supplies and many other products.

## Classified advertising

Relatively few online classified advertising sites seem to have got under way in the UK as yet. It is worth exploring the newsgroups (page 174). A number of new-economy entrepreneurs have made the attempt, though some have fallen by the wayside. The following list includes the leading players.

*AdHunter*
http://www.adhunter.co.uk
This service offers access to classified advertising from around the UK. It is divided into various separate areas. Autohunter then led us to car, bike, boat, caravan and commercial vehicle hunter. In Carhunter alone, there were 143,000 – how could you not find a suitable car! In Jobhunter they had 23,000 jobs advertised on the day we visited, and by the time you read this, there should be Propertyhunter. We really like this site, it is extremely well designed and user friendly.

*BuyStuff*
http://192.41.25.87/oswelcome.shtml
The site offers classified ads and auctions for the UK. It appears to be in its infancy, with few products on offer, though the presentation is clear and attractive.

Shopping for books
A Base for Shoppin
A Base for Shoppin
Free Coupons and
A Base for Free Ma
Free Daily Email Ne
A Base for Women
Free Trial Magazine
A Base for Free Ma
A Base for Teen Fa
A Base for Free Co
All Free Catalogs to
Bluefly - women's,
Buyer's Index - mai
CatalogSite - find a
Catalog Mart -catal
CatalogSite - 100's

# Catalogues, classifieds and auctions.....................................

*E-Mart*

http://www.e-mart.co.uk/

This well-designed net-based trading magazine is overflowing with adverts for different products and is the type of site you *must* visit before venturing down to the shops. You'll find ads for motoring, spares, sundries and a few actual vehicles. A good VW (cut down) was for sale, at a reasonable price, and there was a good motorbike in another section. The real success on this site, and it was extremely good on the day we visited, was the general advertising. There were lots of ads that are well worth browsing.

*Exchange and Mart*

http://www.exchangeandmart.co.uk/

Fig. 28. Exchange & Mart has made a very successful move towards internet sales. The site is full of information on how to search for what you want, and how to place an ad yourself.

The old-established *Exchange & Mart* weekly magazine has forged ahead in using the internet. It runs an online searchable database of classified advertisements drawn from the printed edition. The main sections include Home & Leisure, covering holidays, DIY, gardening and pets; Motor, with over 130,000 cars plus motorbikes, vans, plates, insurance, finance; and Business, where you will find everything from computers to compressors, and other products and services for small businesses everywhere. You can even buy and sell at its live online auction.

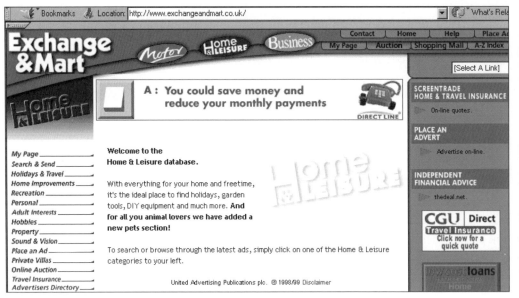

*Industrial Exchange & Mart*

http://www.iem-net.co.uk/

This is a searchable database of classified ads for building materials, industrial machinery, tools, storage, handling, and distribution. Like its sister publication, it offers auctions, offering such things as drilling machines and compressors. It also contains some information about businesses for sale, and exhibitions.

# Catalogues, classifieds and auctions

*Local Ads Net*

http://www.localads.net/

This is an ambitious UK classifieds portal website. It has identified a lo-cally-based market, where people prefer to buy and sell within the local area, perhaps a short drive away. It has around 150 individual town sites attached to it. When you visit the site, a list of these towns is downloaded into your browser window, and you then click on the one you want, and start looking through the ads.

*Loot*

http://www.loot.com/

Loot has established a leading place among the online classified sites. It offers a free online service for private advertisers. You'll find ads for trans-port, computers, household, accommodation and property, hobbies and sports, sound and vision, travel, jobs and personal. There are around 140,000 ads at any one time, and they say that goods to the value of more than £400 million have been advertised. The 3,000 or so personal ads included a section where you can try to find long-lost friends. If you can't find what you're looking for, or you're looking for something speci-fic, then let MySearches search for you. Using the SearchAlert function, Loot can send you an email to tell you how many ads match what you are looking for.

*Net Trader*

http://www.nettrader.co.uk/

We spent ages browsing this site; there was so much good stuff here. It has sections dealing with on the road, property, computers, home and leisure, business, education, web site design and domain name registra-tion.

*Preloved*

http://www.preloved.com/

Preloved is a UK and Ireland database of 'preloved' items. You can buy and sell just about anything here, completely free of charge. It has over 500 categories, with thousands of items from nearly to really old. If you can't find exactly what you're looking, just set an ad Alert, and it will go on tirelessly searching for you, letting you know by email as soon as something suitable turns up. Preloved also enables enthusiasts and col-lectors to get together as an online community. Bargain Banter, its discussion forum, is full of people looking to share their knowledge and experience in buying, selling and maintaining their pride and joy.

*Yahoo! UK Classifieds*

http://uk.classifieds.yahoo.com/uk/

As one would expect of the mighty Yahoo!, this UK and Ireland site is excellent. It is jammed full of goodies, with a large number of adverts for cars, properties for sale and to rent, and job vacancies. The site down-loads quickly, it is concise, easily accessed and full of useful information and opportunities.

# Catalogues, classifieds and auctions........................................

**YAHOO!® CLASSIFIEDS**
UK & IRELAND                 Home - Yahoo! - Help

check your calendar
any where, at any time
**YAHOO!** Calendar
click here, it's FREE!

## Classifieds

**Classifieds Partners**

Partner with Yahoo! Classifieds
Extend your reach.

**Inside Yahoo!**

- Yahoo! Cars - Info on every new car in the UK
- Yahoo! Auctions
- Jobs at Yahoo!
- Yahoo! Shopping
- Yahoo! Business Finder

**Cars**

Research New and Used Cars.
- Car Classifieds
- New Car Information
- Car News

**Employment**

National and International Job Opportunites
- Current vacancies

**Property for Sale**

Search Thousands of Homes Nationally
- Find a new home in your area

**Property for Rent**

Search Rental Property Nationally
- Rentals available now

Fig. 29. The web site of Yahoo! Classifieds which contains thousands of small ads for cars, jobs, and homes for sale and to rent. This is its UK area.

## Auctions

Auction fever is sweeping the internet. The biggest online auction web site of all is eBay, which has auctioned millions of products for millions of dollars. The biggest UK and European one is QXL. Many other web sites are following their lead – even web sites whose main business is completely different. Perhaps auctions, like barter, satisfy some primitive human instinct. The internet has created huge new interest in both types of transaction.

You can bid, not just for traditional auction lots such as collectibles and antiques, but for a mind-boggling array of goods and services of every imaginable kind. Reserve prices are usually shown, mostly in dollars. The auctions have a time limit, normally a few days ahead, and you can see how the bidding has progressed to the current highest bid on the table. Generally there are short descriptions of the lots, and a photograph if the bidder is willing to pay for one. Some sites are strong on customer feedback, which is publicly posted for everyone's benefit.

You will need to register with a site if you intend to be a seller or bidder. In all the excitement, remember to keep your wits about you. Don't forget the practicalities of foreign exchange, credit card security, international shipping costs, insurance, customs clearance, and the possible disappointment if the purchased item fails to live up to your expectations.

*Art and Auction*
http://www.art-auction-annual.com/
This is a starting point for exploring fine art at auction. It claims to be the most complete and detailed art auction data bank online. It covers painting, drawing, sculpture, prints and photography, spanning 155,000 artists' records and 1,650,000 items. You can see where auctions are coming up soon. This is not the easiest of sites to negotiate. If you are

into art it is well worth a look, but you may need to persevere to find what you want.

*Auction Online*
http://www.onsale.com
This is a superbly designed site, and contains some worthwhile bargains. We found some great computer hardware for sale and value-for-money office materials. Make sure you read the bidders' guide first. The site is American and the prices are in dollars, so check out the exchange rate. Also, you need to make sure what shipping charges may come to, so you are not caught out. Remember to set your upper bidding limit and stick to it – there are always plenty more auctions to visit and auction lots to inspect.

*AuctionRover*
http://www.auctionrover.com/
AuctionRover is an auction agent. A bot (piece of software) enables you to conduct searches for items on the leading web auction sites such as eBay and Yahoo!. It then notifies you by email as soon as an item matching your description becomes available.

*AuctionWatch*
http://www.omnibot.com/
This is another useful auction agent site. It helps you manage and monitor lots at different auctions. It is rather unusual in that it concentrates on the more traditional real-world auction houses.

*Auction Watchers*
http://www.auctionwatchers.com/
Auction Watchers allows you to search and also use their advanced search bots to find the best deals on computer equipment currently available from the major online auctions.

*Auctions On-Line*
http://www.auctions-on-line.com/
This is a comprehensive international database of fine art, antiques and collectibles auction information and catalogues. The site is well presented, easy to negotiate, and includes a programme of forthcoming sales. One recent auction featured Elvis personal memorabilia from the Gracelands mansion, combined with links to the official Gracelands web site.

*Auction Talk*
http://www.auctiontalk.com/
This is an essential bookmark – a portal site that links to numerous other sites. The ones we explored were all American, but in this global age this is something to get used to. When the present narrow internet bandwidth is replaced by broadband, we can expect to use sites like this to link very easily and quickly to anywhere on the planet. This may involve a paradigm shift in the thinking and expectations of non-American shoppers, but the

whole world is changing – and shrinking. This site renders a useful service by listing auction-related resources and providing hyperlinks to them.

## Bidder's Edge

http://www.biddersedge.com/

Bidder's Edge can help you find great products, help you work out what to pay, and help you succeed. It provides buying tools and bots for people shopping at online auctions. You can search its database of product and pricing information and personalise these services to your individual needs with some handy features called My Auctions and Deal Watch.

## Bidworth

http://www.bidworth.com/

Bidworth is a tool for person-to-person trading, a new, fun and inexpensive way to buy and sell at auction. The site looks simple enough, but it is clearly laid out and sttraightforward to use. There is practical guidance on what to do, and not to do, and the fees are shown in a handy table. There are no charges to bidders, only sellers. At the end of the auction the seller and the highest bidder each receive an email notifying them of each other's email address, and explaining that they should carry out the deal at the final bid price within three days of the close of the auction. If the buyer refuses to buy the item, the seller advises Bidworth by email and Bidworth will refer the seller to the next highest bidder.

## Bonhams

http://www.bonhams.com/

Bonhams is an old-established British auction house. This is a quality site as befits such a famous name. You don't need to based in London or the south east to gain access to these high quality items. Don't assume that they are out of your price range. For example, there was a beautiful decorative Chinese blue and white vase, painted with deer and crane in a river landscape, with a guide price of £100 to £150. If you enjoy watching programmes like *The Antiques Roadshow* you will enjoy this site.

## Christies

http://www.christies.com/

Christies is another famous old-established London auction house. It is worth looking at their detailed and expert advice on how to buy and sell at auction. When reviewed, the site featured an auction of collectible cars at rather serious prices. They also have a highly regarded educational sector in which you can learn more about fine art. A visit here could enhance your appreciation of the finer things in life.

## eBay

http://www.ebay.com/

This is the world's biggest and best known online auction site. It is a place to find both collectibles and the more mundane things in life. You can buy and sell items in more than 1,000 categories, including collectibles, antiques, sports memorabilia, computers, toys, beanies, dolls, figures,

Fig. 30. eBay is without question the world's biggest and best-known online auction supermarket, and selling and bidding at such auctions has become something of a craze.

coins, stamps, books, magazines, music, pottery, glass and many others. For example, you might come across a rare signed copy of *To Kill A Mocking Bird* by Harper Lee, or a set of 1960s *Organic Gardening* magazines, or a classic motor car. More than a million items of every kind are constantly on offer, often at very low disclosed reserves. Be warned, it can become very addictive.

*Global Auction*
http://www.global-auction.com/
The most appealing aspect of this site, when you arrive, is that they say everything is free. The information is quite good. For example, in the collectibles section you will find a written description of the item and often a photograph. Some of the objects on offer were somewhat tacky. Well, taste is a personal matter. Before you buy anything from an overseas auction house, check whether or not any duties are payable: it could add to the cost of your bargain. In the UK you could phone your local Customs and Excise Office for advice.

*Internet Auction List*
http://www.internetauctionlist.com/
This is a web portal to some massive listings of online auctions, and it just shows what an enormously popular activity this is becoming all over the world. You'll find a wealth of information here, and details of getting to other sites where auctions are held. The page downloads are rather slow, but the information is worth the wait.

*Internet Shopping Network*
http://www.internet.net/
Why not explore one of the web's most exciting retail auction sites, where you can place bids on everything from housewares to collectibles, music

and computers? The auctions are organised around categories such as electronics, golf equipment, healthy living and beauty. There are about twenty 30-minute auctions each day, and 48-hour auctions starting every day. Bidding can often start at a rock bottom one dollar, though some goods start off a little higher.

*Klik-Klok Dutch Auction*

http://www.klik-klok.com/auction.html

This is an excellent example of the 'Dutch auction' in practice. You have only a limited time to view the product – about two minutes – and then you start bidding. In a Dutch auction the bids go down rather than up. The risk is that you may wait for the price to fall very low, only to find that it is suddenly sold to someone else and is withdrawn. The Dutch style of auction can be as tense as any other, though the concept is probably alien to many British bidders. There is a phone number on the site, so you can talk to a real person if you wish.

*Loot Auctions*

http://www.loot.com/

Loot began as a UK classified advertising medium, but is now offering online auctions as well. Click the auction link on its home page, to view an enormous list of around 10,000 items for which bids are invited. Reserve prices are shown, and the number of days left to the close of each auction, for example two or three days. A small percentage of the items are illustrated alongside the brief details. If you register on the site, the benefits will include being able to sell items free, auction for free, bid for free, save your searches, and use the Search Alert and My Clipboard facilities. The site includes some detailed FAQs to explain the procedures.

*Online Auction House*

http://on-line-auction.com/

This site requires registration, though it is free. Submitting your details makes you a target for their marketing, whether by snail mail or email. We were impressed by the sales advice offered here to sellers. If you are new to selling at auction, clear practical explanations are vital. There was an impressive array of stores here, where you could get 50 per cent off the price of purchased items. The biggest category was computer and video games (about 700 items) followed by collectibles (about 400 items).

*Onsale*

http://www.onsale.com

To bid at this site, you must first fill out a fairly long registration page. Visa is the preferred method of payment. Bidders must enter a user name and password, which are used each time a bid is made. You can enter bids for computer products, software, printers, sports equipment and travel products. A useful feature is its express auctions. These open at only $1 and run from 9am to 8pm (PDT) everyday, including weekends. New items are listed every day.

## QXL
http://www.qxl.com/

The British publicly-quoted company QXL is the best-known European-based online auction site. The name is derived from 'quick sell'. You may find hardware goods being offered from as little as £1. Make sure you know what the bid increments are. In some cases it might be £1, in other cases £25. A £25 increment means that the item is going up by £25 a time, even if it starts off at £1.

## Sothebys
http://www.sothebys.com/

This is a delightful site, as befits the famous Bond Street firm of auctioneers and valuers. Sothebys have entered into a joint agreement with Amazon, the online bookstore, to establish an online auction house. This is an intriguing ten-year alliance between the old world and the new. The two companies were established 251 years apart. The joint site will provide opportunities for dealers in collectibles to sell in a marketplace with unparalleled reach. Sellers will also be able to market to Amazon's 10 million strong customer base.

## Winebid
http://www.winebid.com

If you are in the wine profession, or a keen amateur, this very professional-looking site is an essential bookmark. Wherever you are in the world, you can bid for some of the finest wines produced. It's rather like a futures market, in that you can buy wines that have yet to be bottled. Auctions are held in the USA, Australia and UK. A commission of 12.5 per cent is charged on each sale. When the wine is ready for shipping, customers are contacted to arrange the delivery method and payment. If you

Fig. 31. If you want a UK-based alternative to eBay's online auctions, then QXL ('Quick Sell') is probably your best bet. It has established itself as the European market leader.

65

# Catalogues, classifieds and auctions.....................................

Bookmarks   Netsite: http://www.sothebys.com/    What's Re

## SOTHEBYS.COM

AUCTIONS ONLINE   AUCTION HOUSE   SOTHEBY'S CONNOISSEUR   CALENDAR   SHOP SOTHEBY'S   SOTHEBY'S SERVICES   ABOUT SOTHEBY'S   SITE SEARCH

Log In | Register | Help

**Auctions Online**

SPECIAL AUCTIONS
PAINTINGS, DRAWINGS & WATERCOLORS
SCULPTURE
PRINTS
PHOTOGRAPHS
JEWELRY
WATCHES & CLOCKS
FURNITURE
RUGS & TEXTILES
CERAMICS & GLASS
SILVER
BOOKS & MANUSCRIPTS
COLLECTIBLES
OTHER PROPERTY
BROWSE ALL CATEGORIES

**Sotheby's Connoisseur**

COLLECTING GUIDES
AUCTION LINK
EDUCATION AT SOTHEBY'S

CLOCKS & BAROMETERS

A DRAWING BY JOHN SINGER SARGENT
OFFERED BY DANIEL HUNT FINE ART

In the
**Auction House**

CALENDAR
CATALOGUES
COLLECTING DEPARTMENTS

SPECIAL AUCTIONS ONLINE

**SOTHEBYS**
› International Realty
› Financial Services

Fig. 32. Sotheby's is now online. This fascinating site helps to demystify the world of top antique furniture, paintings and prints, ceramics, silver, watches, jewellery and other fine collectibles available at auction.

are happy to buy your Cabernet Sauvignon from the local supermarket, this may not be for you, but if you are serious about wine, this is well worth exploring. The site includes a downloadable catalogue, auction results, wineries direct, an auction calendar, and the facility to track your consignment.

*Yahoo! Auctions*
http://auctions.yahoo.com/
This is the auction site of the giant internet search engine. As with many of these auction sites, it is American, so exchange rates, import duties and shipping costs may all impact on how much you are prepared to offer. The site contains a huge array of items. Remember that many of the goods on offer will have been designed for American and not European use.

*ZDNet Auctions*
http://auctions.zdnet.com/
Last but not least is another American site, from internet market leader Ziff-Davis. This site is packed with intriguing items. Like a growing number of similar sites, it has an 'auction agent'. By registering what you are looking for, this does the browsing for you automatically. Have a good look around before you start bidding. There is an excellent FAQ (frequently asked questions) section, which you should not miss. Read their advice for both buyers and sellers, regardless of which role you intend to play.

# 5 Shops and stores

**In this chapter we will explore:**

▶ *UK shops and stores*
▶ *UK shopping centres*
▶ *international shopping*

. . . . . . . . . . . . . . . . . . . . . . . . . . . . . . . . . . . . . . . . . . . . . . . . . . . . . . . . . . . . . . . . . . . . . . . . . . . . . . . . . . . . . . .

## UK shops and stores

Most leading UK retail companies are now developing web sites, although there are still some surprising omissions. Online retailers vary a great deal in what they offer and how they offer it. Some load their pages with flashy graphics that convey little practical information, and just slow down your internet experience. Some seem to consider their web site as little more than a glorified brochure. Others are clearly making a substantial bid for long-term business online.

A good 'etailer' will offer fast-downloading pages and clear navigation, so you aren't tempted to click away. Product information should be concise and easy to find, with clear details of colours, sizes and prices, and enlargeable images to click on so you can get a good picture of what you are buying. Telephone helplines and catalogue requests forms are very useful. Terms of trade should be easy to ascertain – delivery time and costs, arrangements for exchanges and refunds, credit and debit cards accepted, and whether you can also order offline by fax, post or phone. The shopping cart should use fully secure technology, and enable you to drop in or remove any of its contents until the last moment.

*Allders*
http://www.allders.co.uk
Allders operates 36 household stores nationwide with sales of around £500m a year. Its web site is divided into products, stores, customer services, corporate and feedback, with further sections on women's clothing and home furnishings. You can also be added to the Allders mailing list. If you see something you like on their site you will need to contact your local shop for further details. A list of department stores and at home stores in various locations in provided. The site provides some information and photos of goods for sale, and of the Allders' wedding gift service and account card.

*Asda*
http://www.asda.co.uk
Asda is one of the biggest chains of grocery and housewares superstores in the UK, and is now a division of the US retail giant Walmart. You can explore what's new, feedback, food talk, store finder, and job vacancies at Asda. There is information on having books, videos and CDs delivered directly to your home: a telephone number but no email address is pro-

vided for this. The site offers advice about nutrition, vegetarianism and vegetarian recipes, diabetes and diet information for diabetics, but when reviewed there was no information about shopping online.

### BHS (British Home Stores)
http://www.bhs.co.uk
The home page of BHS, the chain of British Home Stores, said 'coming soon'. BHS is part of the Storehouse retail group.

### Blacks
http://www.blacks.co.uk
Blacks Leisure Group specialises in outdoor footwear, clothing and equipment. The opening page is graphics heavy and takes time to download. Click Products to find out more about sleeping bags, outdoor clothing, tents, walking shoes, rucksacks and ski equipment. Frustratingly, clicking photos of the products doesn't enable you to access information on sizes, colours, and prices. Clicking Stores just brings up a photograph of the outside of a Blacks store but doesn't tell you how to find one.

SEARCH THE SITE
- ● articles
- ○ mother & baby shop
- ○ health & beauty shop
- sunglasses   go!

SITE TOOLS
- • site help
- • feedback
- • sitemap

Site legal terms
Customer charter
About your privacy
Advantage card

*Boots*
*Advantage Card*

### Boots the Chemist
http://www.boots.co.uk
Boots is the UK's best-known chain of high street chemists. On its web site you'll find sections for help, register, email, contacts, library and information. On the contacts page you can find a list of addresses and phone numbers for advice on topics such as pre-pregnancy and pregnancy, home doctor and lifestyle. Each is conveniently arranged into sub-topics such as family planning, fertility, disorders, eczema, drinking, smoking, and accidents. You can email Boots with feedback.

### British Heart Foundation Shops
http://www.bhf.org.uk/shops/zindex.html
The BHF has over 300 charity shops throughout the UK and Northern Ireland. Its site explains how you can make a donation in the form of second hand clothes, books and bric-a-brac. You can also find out how to become a BHF volunteer. Click a small map of the UK (divided into nine regions) to explore local news, events, support groups and volunteering. The site is clear, informative and easy to navigate.

### Clarks
http://www.clarks.co.uk/
Clarks is an old-established shoe manufacturer and retailer, with a chain of shops across the UK. Key in your postcode to find details of your nearest stockists. The site includes a virtual shoesizer to help you work out your correct shoe size. There is a brief history of the company, including the desert boot for which Clarks was famous.

### Comet UK
http://www.comet.co.uk
The Comet chain of superstores sells a big range of consumer electrical

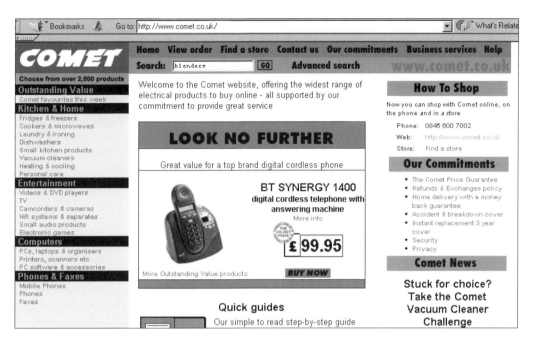

Fig. 33. Electrical retailer
Comet offers its wide
range of products for sale
online.

appliances, from kitchen and household to entertainment, PCs, communications and personal care products. The site explains how to order, and
how to locate the nearest Comet store with the aid of a store finder,
printable map and store address (other companies take note!). You can
look up the arrangements for refunds, exchanges, warranties, after-sales
service, and Comet's price promise. Each household section contains a
wealth of information with product names, descriptions and prices.

*Co-op*
http://www.co-op.co.uk
The Co-op offers a bright, well-designed site with few graphics. It tells
you about Co-op advertising, co-operative funeral services, vegetarianism and community dividends. For information about its latest internet-
based services, check out its online sales page. This will tell you about
internet banking, cooperative insurance, travel services, shopping for domestic appliances, tax-free ISAs, and how to order wines by the case.
Background information is offered on honest labelling and animal testing.

*Debenhams*
http://www.debenhams.co.uk
Debenhams is an established chain of UK high street department stores.
Its home page has links to department information, what's new, its wedding service and corporate services, magazine and customer services.
There are departments for women, men, children and the home, sport,
and designers. Click a topic to view colour photographs and the prices of
selected articles. A store locator helps you find the nearest store by clicking the first letter of your town name.

# Shops and stores.............................................

*Dixons*
http://www.dixons.co.uk/
Dixons Online enables you to browse, select and buy photographic goods, computer supplies, hi-fi, television and video players, communications, software, games, accessories and personal care equipment. Within each category there are sub-categories. For example, under photography there are cameras, binoculars, camcorders, and film supplies. Click a sub-topic to see product models and descriptions, prices and other details. You must register in order to shop online. All personal and credit card information is encrypted before transmission so that you can shop safely. Dixons owns the PC World computer stores, and founded Freeserve, the UK internet service provider.

*Dollond and Aitchison*
http://www.danda.co.uk
This site takes a while to download. Once it does, take a look at Personal Eyes, a service that enables you to try on different spectacle frames. You will need to scan in a photograph of yourself and upload it to their web site. A demonstration is available for people who are unwilling or unable to upload photos. Just choose a face from the gallery and select a spectacle frame. There is also a page with an online form for careers enquiries.

*Fortnum & Mason*
http://www.fortnumandmason.co.uk
This is the web site of the famous London Piccadilly store and Royal Warrant holder, supplier to the pantries and larders of English homes since the early eighteenth century. It offers some tempting online shopping for luxury food and drink items. Among the many goodies on show are hampers, chocolates, fines wines, champagne, and various exquisite gastronomic gifts.

*Great Universal Stores*
http://www.shoppersuniverse.com
Shoppers Universe brings you the top high-street brand names from lingerie and clothing to sports and technical equipment. The site downloads quickly. Under Net Sale you should find information about sales in ladies fashion, men's casual wear, girls' and boys' clothing, jewellery and housewares. Toy Town covers dolls and accessories, Teletubbies, skating and bikes, and music and entertainment (among others). Click the name of an item to view a photograph, a brief description and price. This is a massive and very professionally produced site, offering around 40,000 products.

*Harrods*
http://www.harrods.com/
In its distinctive colours of jade green and black, the Harrods home page leads you to factual and historical information about the famous department store in London's Knightsbridge. Harrods has been a magnet for overseas visitors for generations, and it is famous for its seasonal sales. To start online shopping, you read the product details by moving your

pointer over your selected images. Click on these to begin the purchase process, which leads you to the checkout area. The range of items appeared fairly limited, but the site is still in an early stage of development. When reviewed, shipping appeared to be available to USA and Canada addresses only.

*High & Mighty*
http://www.high-mighty.co.uk
High and Mighty is a fashion retailer for big and tall men. Its site tells you about the High and Mighty account, methods of payment, what's new, company information, finding your local branch and getting hold of a brochure. There is a selection of suits, shirts, casual jackets, nightwear, underwear, footwear, accessories and other items, with reference numbers and prices. Click on the individual product photographs to get details of sizes and prices, before moving to the online shopping cart and checkout. Alternatively, you can order by fax or post. There is information on how to find the nearest High and Mighty shop in the UK or on the continent.

*Homebase*
http://www.homebase.co.uk
The site is divided into sections with names such as home, the space race, at home with art, in working order, 20 fabulous things, and the environment. We found the navigation of the site is somewhat confusing: if you click about the house, entry pages for the Space Race and Twenty Fabulous Things appear. Space Race shows storage boxes, cupboards and cabinets with accompanying information on how to do the interior decoration. Twenty Fabulous Things is actually twenty buys all under £20. These are wallpapers and accompanying borders, tile transfers, picture frames and CD racks.

*Ikea*
http://www.ikea.co.uk
They say: 'At this time we do not have a national web site, but for now we invite you to visit the IKEA global site and locate the store nearest you. To find out which national sites have been launched, check out the What's New section in the IKEA global site.' They have many European web sites, but at the time of review no UK web site.

*JD Sports*
http://www.jdsports.co.uk
Click the news button to see photographs (but no information on sizes or prices) on the latest trainers. Or, by answering a simple question, you can enter a competition to win a sports prize. The Cybershop page enables you to buy your favourite football team's shirt. Or, if you prefer to visit JDSports in person simply click a region of the UK map for details of your nearest shop to be displayed. If you don't see what you want, or have further questions, you can fill in an online form and ask.

# Shops and stores.............................................................

Fig. 34. The web site of JD Sports, the well-known UK high street retailer.

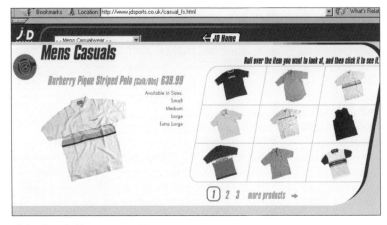

### John Lewis Department Stores
http://www.johnlewis.co.uk
This is the place to find out about the Waitrose grocery store, John Lewis stores and the John Lewis Partnership. At Waitrose you can buy wine online, and there are plans to offer organic food and flowers as well.

### Maplins
http://www.maplin.co.uk/

Fig. 35. As a top supplier of electronic goods, Maplin has an impressive online retail store. Remember to check out its latest special offers.

Maplins sells electrical and electronic products such as aerials, amplifiers, batteries, chargers and accessories, filters, suppression and EMC and fixings and hardware. Pass your cursor over the various categories – products, help, about us, ordering – and a menu is displayed. The site is well organised, and includes FAQs and a keyword search. Under pro-

ducts you will see catalogue browse, multi-product ordering and promotions. About Us offers history, latest news, publications, contact information, company profile and job information. Click on ordering to see the site map, conditions of sale and export, UK mail order, retail sites and online catalogue ordering. Maplins leads the way by making full use of online security from the moment you enter the site.

*Marks and Spencer*
http://www.marks-and-spencer.com/
M & S has struggled in Britain's high streets in the last two or three years, and it will be interesting to see whether online retailing marks a turn in its fortunes. Its site tells you about its stores worldwide, London visitor information, and customer services. There is a handy map on how to find the flagship Marble Arch store, a list of services and a diagram of what you'll find on each floor. Its growing range of online products are well organised, illustrated (with enlargeable images) and clearly priced. You can now order from its online checkout. Remember to make a selection of size and colour first. There is also an email update service.

*Past Times Shops*
http://www.pasttimes.com
Past Times offers a selection of imaginative gifts inspired by different epochs in history. Most are authentic replicas or based on period designs. The site opens with a list of shop addresses and telephone numbers. It tells you about ordering by phone in the UK, USA, France and Japan, or by post from anywhere in the world, or by visiting any of the shops listed . You can ask for a catalogue online.

*PC World*
http://www.pcworld.co.uk
This is the online home of PC World computer stores – a company probably more responsible than any other for getting the people of Britain online in the last couple of years. Its breezily presented site offers four

Fig. 36. The retail web site of PC World. Even if you don't buy from here, it would be a good idea to browse the online store for product specifications and prices before you visit the real thing.

73

main shopping areas: software, hardware, furniture and downloads. Once you have found what you want, click Add to Basket, or Buy Now. If you want to go on shopping, look for the Return to Store button on the bottom menu bar. You can change the contents of your basket until the moment you are ready to pay. They say that orders placed by 3pm will be dispatched within one working day, subject to stock availability, and that there is delivery charge of £3.25 per order. Delivery is within the UK mainland only.

*Post Office Counters*
http://www.postoffice-counters.co.uk
The site is divided into personal and business services, information about going abroad, what's new and thumbnail information about weather and latest news. The services offered are bureau de change (soon to be operational on the web site), and everyday insurance cover. Visitors will find the postage calculator useful for working out the cost of sending letters, packages and parcels anywhere in the world. Other useful facilities are track and trace for post within the UK, a postcode look-up, and a map to indicate your nearest post office.

*Toys R Us*
http://www.toysrus.co.uk
Toys R Us has a giant web site. Its online catalogue offers around 1,000 products – toys, video games, multimedia, outdoor and consumer electronics such as TVs and videos. There are displays of the latest promotions and offers, and details of its home delivery service. A drop-down menu on the home page enables you to search by department (action toys, fashion dolls, Star Wars and so on). Alternatively, you can use Toy Finder by entering the name of a toy and the maximum price you want to pay. You can jump from here to selected toy manufacturers' web sites such as Hornby, Scalextric, Nintendo and Mattel.

*Woolworths*
http://www.woolworths.co.uk
Part of the Kingfisher retail group, and a long-term survivor in the retail market, Woolworths remains a UK leader in children's clothes, entertainment, toys and confectionery. Its 800 stores attract almost a million customers every day, sell around 20 million Easter eggs and 14 million books each year, and 3,000 mobile phones a week. The product offerings on the site were still fairly limited when reviewed, but the site does benefit from a secure server. Just complete the online order form and choose how you want to pay. The site accepts Visa, Mastercard, Switch, Delta and Solo Cards. It explains about delivery arrangements and refunds.

### UK shopping centres

*Bicester Village*
http://www.bicester-village.co.uk/
Bicester Village in Oxfordshire is an 'outlet mall'. Here you'll find about 60

shops, many of them representing famous brand merchandise such as Paul Smith, Versace, Waterford Wedgwood, Benetton, Ralph Lauren and many others. They specialise in offering previous season and end-of-line goods with big price reductions. You can click arrows to see samples of store offerings and the outlet site.

*Granary Wharf*
http://www.granary-wharf.co.uk
The Granary Wharf shopping centre is in Leeds, Yorkshire. Its shops offer a wide variety of goods from clothing to didgeridoos, stained glass, and fine wines. The site showed phone numbers, but no individual shop hyperlinks.

*Jermyn Street*
http://www.jermynstreet.com
Thanks to the internet, London's fashionable Jermyn Street is accessible to all. Its retailers and other businesses are listed in street order and shown on a handy map. The site provides a listing of theatres and places to eat, as well as phone numbers and addresses. If you are not sure where to start, explore the categories listing which puts everything from antique rugs to virtual offices at your fingertips. It also has details of opening times, weather, exchange rates, and public transport.

*Meadowhall*
http://www.meadowhall.co.uk
Meadowhall is a huge shopping centre in Sheffield, Yorkshire. The web site tells you all about shopping here, customer services, gift certificates, membership cards, crèches, and birthday parties. You can find audiovisual and photographic goods, cards and gifts, children's wear, fashion accessories, financial services, food stores, footwear, hairdressing, health and beauty, home furnishings and fabrics, jewellery, ladies' and men's wear, news, stationery and books, opticians, specialist shops and services, sports and outdoor leisure goods, toys and games, travel agents, restaurants and fast food outlets, and a simple map of the malls

*Milton Keynes*
http://www.cmkshop.co.uk/
This page is part of the Milton Keynes web site. The shopping centre has over 200 stores to choose from, among them Body Shop, Boots, Superdrug, Next, Mothercare, Thorntons, and Whittard of Chelsea. Just click the section you are interested in and then the specific store to see where it is. You will find chemists and cosmetics, children's clothing, confectionery and gift goods, estate agents, fashion accessories, hairdressing, jewellery and watches. Viewing the online store plan could help you plan a worthwhile day out.

*Royal Victoria*
http://propertymall.com/rvp/
Royal Victoria is a mall in Tunbridge Wells, Kent. The shops are listed A to Z, and include florists, food stores and fashion. There is a brief description

of each, and a floor plan to show how to get to it. The services offered include customer liaison, car parking, security, crèche, and a special eating area for children. The site has a map of how to get there.

*White Rose Shopping Mall*
http://www.white-rose.co.uk
White Rose lies four miles south west of Leeds. There are more than 100 retail outlets to explore here, ranging from fashion and beauty through to travel agents and restaurants. With all the major high street names under one roof, there is something for everyone. The site offers an informative and entertaining newsletter on what is happening. You can also read some fashion tips and get advice on what sunscreen to pack before jetting off to the sun.

## International shopping

*Bloomingdale's*
http://www.bloomingdale's.com
Fancy a shopping trip to New York's Manhattan? This is the quick-loading web site of the world-famous Lexington Avenue store. The opening page takes you to Just In, B-search, Shopping, Bridal Registry, In Store, and About. Some visitors may need to adjust their screens to sign up for b-mail since the box for submitting an email address is cut off. In Just In, you can investigate Bloomingdale's latest basement sale and special offers. You can also set up your own personal online shopping profile.

Fig. 37. Have you ever longed to visit some of Manhattan's famous stores? Bloomingdales is now available online.

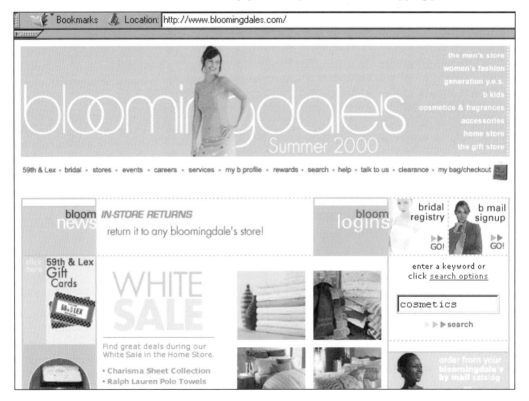

*Canada Yellow Pages*
http://www.canadayellowpages.com
The site incorporates listings, news and general information, and benefits from links to a number of similar yellow pages sites around the world

*Disney Store Online*
http://www.disney.com/shop
The home page offers information on shopping, holidays, a chat studio, Disney A to Z, movies, television programmes, pets and animals and fun for families. You can search for topics such as entertainment, books, Disney interactive and home video. A third pull-down menu displays corporate news, Disney careers and educational programmes. Under shopping there is a gift centre and special offers. To access some of the features, however, you need Disney membership, for example to enter contests and sweepstakes, and take part in bulletin boards.

*Dutch Yellow Pages*
http://www.markt.nl/dyp/
This efficient site lists commercial organisations in Amsterdam, the Hague, Rotterdam, Utrecht and other parts of the Netherlands. Look for the link on the left of the window to read the site in English.

*Galéries Lafayette*
http://www.galerieslafayette.com/
How about a shopping trip to Paris? This is the web site of the famous French department store: 'Grand magasin, boutique de cadeaux, listes de mariage, mode, conseils beauté et services du magasin Haussmann.' Reflecting the online global market, the site can also be read in English and Japanese.

Fig. 38. The shops of Paris are just a few mouse clicks away. This is the web site of Galeries Lafayette, famous for its fashionwear and accessories

# Shops and stores..............................................

*Hong Kong Yellow Pages*
http://www.yp.com.hk/english/
Launched in 1997, this online database brings together around 300,000 Hong Kong companies arranged in 1,800 classifications. Free public information, including useful local hotlines and links to other directories in the world, is also available for easy reference.

*Irish Internet Yellow Pages*
http://www.nci.ie/Yellow/
This is an online directory of Irish businesses searchable by region or category. The entries include fax numbers, mobile phone numbers, web pages (where they exist) and other useful data. A search for antique dealers in Dublin, for example, turned up 19 entries.

*Italian Shops*
http://www.visit.it
This is the Vatican art souvenir web site, which takes a while to download. On offer are religious gifts, mementoes for the Year 2000 Jubilee, books and multimedia on Italian and Catholic themes and art. There is a search engine which enables you to go directly to Papal blessing parchments, rosaries, crosses, medals of Christ, medals of Mary, a poster of Pope John Paul II and crucifixes. You can sign up for the free newsletter, too.

Fig. 39. Even shopping in Japan is easy now, with access to a web site like Japan Yellow Pages. All the old barriers of foreign languages and pricing are rapidly being overcome on the internet.

*Japan Yellow Pages*
http://www.yellowpage-jp.com/info/index.htm
Japan Yellow Pages is a general directory of businesses and services, published twice a year in June and December. Published in English, it includes over 28,000 listings covering hundreds of Japanese industries and businesses.

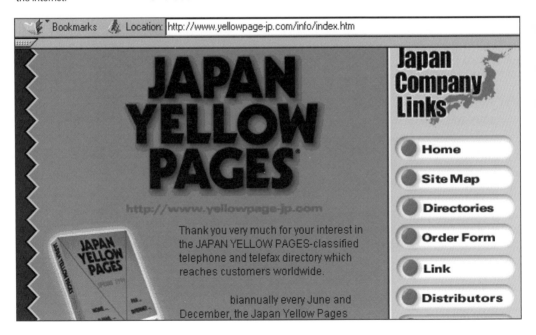

*JC Penney*
http://www.jcpenney.com
JC Penney is a large, well-known US department store. Visit its site to get hold of a catalogue, and find out about their customer services and gift registry. There are weekly offers such as a St John's Bay printed polo shirt, Nike Air walking shoes and Arizona Jean Co quad-pocket pants. The featured departments are clothing, toys, home and leisure, jewellery and specialty shops. Pass your cursor over a category, and a sub-list appears, listing the various items available. A thumbnail photograph of each one is provided with the accompanying price.

*Macy's*
http://www.macys.com
Macy's is a big department store in New York, always full of bargains. You can browse through various pages to explore home furnishings, men's and women's clothing, lingerie, jewellery, accessories, cosmetics and fragrances. Enter your email address to sign up for the Macy's newsletter. You can shop by department and speciality shop, request a catalogue or see what's on sale, and what's new. Use the keyword search to browse by vendor, category and price or use the Product Wizard to find what you want.

Fig. 40. Macy's is probably the world's most famous department store, long established in Manhattan, New York.

*Made in Denmark*
http://www.made-in-denmark.dk/
This English-language site offers direct access to Danish companies and products.

# Shops and stores...................................................

Fig. 41. If you want to shop Australian-style, check out MyShop, which puts thousands of Australian retailers at your fingertips.

*Myshop Australia*
http://www.myshop.com.au/directory.htm
Myshop is a useful directory of Australian online shops, shown under various product categories.

*Neiman Marcus*
http://www.neimanmarcus.com/
Neiman Marcus combines Neiman Marcus Stores, Bergdorf Goodman, and NM Direct. It is a high-end specialty retailer offering women's and men's apparel, fashion and home accessories, shoes, cosmetics, furs, jewellery, and gourmet food products.

*Pagine Gialle*
http://www.paginegialle.it/
This is the web site for Italy's online yellow pages. How about planning a shopping trip to Rome, Florence or Venice?

*Printemps*
http://www.printemps.fr/
Printemps is one of the best-known department stores in France: 'Grand magasin: la mode femme, homme et enfant, la maison, la beauté, les loisirs, une boutique de cadeaux et les listes de mariage'.

*Saks Fifth Avenue*
http://www.saksincorporated.com/
Saks Fifth Avenue is an old-established regional US department store company. It offers middle to top level brand name fashion wear, cosmetics, shoes, accessories and home furnishings.

*Singapore Warehouse Sale*
http://www.warehousesale.com.sg/
This bargain-oriented site includes a listing of companies offering goods for sale at trade prices. It offers all kinds of things from oriental handicrafts to electronics, plus various warehouse links, business directories and more.

*Swiss Yellow Pages*
http://www.pages-jaunes.ch/
The site can be read in English, French, German and Italian.

*Taiwan Yellow Pages*
http://www.yellowpage.com.tw/
This is a handy and well-classified English-language guide to all kinds of value for money products, manufacturers, suppliers and business services from one of the great bargain centres of Asia/

*Walmart*
http://www.walmart.com
An American company, Walmart, is the world's biggest retailer, with subsidiaries all over the world (including Asda in the UK). It offers appliances and homeware, a baby shop, books, computers and software, electronics and cameras, gifts and collectibles, gourmet food, health and medical products, music and video, sports goods and toys. Each product is accompanied by a small photograph, short description and price details. Click the item to view a larger photograph.

# 6 Music, videos, games and toys

**In this chapter we will explore:**

▶ *music*
▶ *video and DVD*
▶ *computer games*
▶ *children's toys*

## Music

### 101cd.com
http://www.101cd.com/
With the recent addition of 500,000 import CDs and music titles, 101cd claims to have over a million CDs, DVDs, videos, games and books in its catalogue, all at discount prices. The site can be viewed in several different European languages and has a range of functional search options, plus a very useful help section, which answers questions on such matters as returns and refunds, and orders and how they are processed.

### Britannia Video & Music Club
http://www.britanniamusic.co.uk/
The latest music recordings and a huge back catalogue of albums are available through Britannia Music Club. The monthly magazine has regular features on the best in pop, rock, indie, dance and soul. With thousands of albums to choose from there's plenty to suit everyone's tastes. To join Britannia Music select any five titles and then buy another six regular priced recordings during your first two years of membership.

### British Audio Dealers Association
http://www.bada.co.uk

BADA represents 125 hi-fi specialist shops in the UK. The site provides a map to click to find the nearest BADA dealer. There is also a BADA free advice web page in case you are not happy with your existing system or uncertain about what upgrade to use. The site also offers ex-demonstration and second hand equipment for sale with details of condition, price, name of retailer and telephone number. The site has links to BADA members and offers guidelines for visitors buying equipment for the first time.

### HMV International
http://www.hmv.co.uk
This site crowds rather a lot onto the home page. Goods are divided into categories such as soul, sound tracks, jazz, easy listening, country, roots, classical singles, videos and games, with an accompanying search engine. There is a list of CDs and videos on sale at £9.99. You can check out the site to see information on the latest audio, singles, games and video new releases. You can join a monthly mailing list for details of new releases. There is a secure online credit card ordering facility.

Fig. 42. Jungle has become one of the best-known UK online suppliers of music, games and videos.

*Jungle.com*
http://www.jungle.com
Identifiable by its yellow and green cartoon snake, Jungle is a prominent online retailer of computers, videos, games, and music (see below under Computer Games).

*Music Boulevard*
http://www.musicblvd.com
This site is divided into news and reviews, sales and specials, gifts, my CD now, and help. There is a search engine with a drop-down list to help you find music by your favourite artist, album or song title, record label, movie title and actor/actress. Music is listed under rock, hip-hop, world, classical sound tracks and other categories. You can also see the latest movie and video releases and buy gift certificates. Thee site offers various incentives and reward points.

## Videos and DVD

*Black Star Videos*
http://www.blackstar.co.uk/
Black Star sell video titles currently on release the UK, covering film, TV, music and sport. They say that if you use their secure transaction procedures, and any unauthorised credit-card purchases are made in conjunction with that use, it will refund the amount not covered by your credit card provider. 'Since we began trading we have not experienced one instance of credit card fraud resulting from information passed to us.' If you are still unsure about sending your details over the web, you can order by phone, fax or post. The site gives details of its returns policy, gift-wrapping service, free postage, and gift certificates.

# Music, videos, games and toys.............................................

*Britannia Video*
http://www.britannia-video.co.uk
Britannia Video Club claims to be the largest video supplier by mail order in Europe. All the latest videos are available through its video club as well as a huge selection of classic films, comedy, children's, special interest, sport and family entertainment. To join you have to choose four recordings, and then buy a further six regular priced recordings during your first two years of membership (at least three of them in your first year).

Fig. 43. Do you want to find that elusive 1980s pop video, or a film by Fellini or Hitchcock? It's easy to find what you want at an online UK store like Choices Direct.

*Choices Direct (formerly Video Plus)*
http://www.choicesdirect.co.uk/
This well presented Peterborough-based site contains over 25,000 video, DVD and talking tapes. You can find details of stars, directors, and production years. There are 19 major categories including foreign films, television, sport, music, readings and many more. New release information is updated daily. You can use the advance search facility to find exactly what you're looking for. You can pay by American Express, MasterCard, Switch or Visa. Orders are accepted both online and by fax.

*Filmworld*
http://www.filmworld.co.uk/
For the more dedicated filmgoer, London-based Filmworld offers in-depth movie and film information, as well as video and DVD sales. 'Whether you want to buy a video/DVD, or you want to check out the reviews and see what's on at your local cinema – or you are a young filmmaker and would want to be part of the FilmWorld network – we want to offer you all that you need right here.' The site includes a video exchange service, trailers, streaming video, film books and posters, and industry news and gossip. You can order products by freephone, fax, post, or online using their secure server.

*McNo*
http://www.mcno.com
McNo has around 500 video CD titles in stock. These include movies, children's titles, music, reference, sports, karaoke and adult. If you are looking for a specific title there is a search facility. All orders over a certain amount entitle you to a free disc: see the latest releases and offers section of the web site for more. All items listed here are normally despatched the same day as receipt of order, by international first class recorded delivery. If you want a catalogue, you will need to send an email stating which category you want.

*Movie Zone*
http://www.moviezone.co.uk
This is a guide to Movie Zone stores and video rental release schedules in the UK.

*Odeon Filmstore*
http://www.filmstore.co.uk/
You can search here by title, actor and director. You can buy the latest releases, pre order new releases in advance of their release date to ensure that you get them on the day of release. Odeon has a substantial back catalogue of other movies, most of them not available locally. They will be adding film soundtracks and other film related merchandise to the site. You can pay by credit card or Switch card using its secure server. The total value of your shopping basket will be displayed together the calculated delivery cost. If you submit an email address and password, you can use its online order tracking service. Alternatively you can speak to an operator who can take your order over the telephone, or you can order by fax.

*Picture Paradise*
http://www.pictureparadise.co.uk/
The site offers region 1 DVDs, previously viewed laserdiscs, and movie memorabilia. It also supplies speakers, amplifiers, projectors, cables and other home cinema equipment. You may need to contact them by phone for further information and ordering.

*Video City*
http://www.videocity.co.uk/
Video City is based in Highgate, London, and was established in 1983. Its DVDs are region 2 coded, and delivered free in the UK. They are available to rent and buy. You must have cookies enabled in your browser. Prices range from around £15.99 to £19.99 and cover action, comedy, horror and science fiction. You will need to type in details of your order, including credit card details, onto the online order form and click Submit. The site does not appear to use encryption technology for transaction processing.

*Video Empire*
http://www.videoempire.com/
With over 20,000 new, used and rare video films on the site – and a

further 40,000 on its database there's a vast choice here. A drop down menu gives quick access to many different genres, plus links to search, service, a wants list, video formats, customer service, contact us, and home. You can enter your email address and click Submit to receive their newsletter. This newsletter will tell you about special offers, forthcoming releases and other important movie information. You must have cookies enabled in your browser. You can offer to sell them your used videos, CDs and DVDs.

*Video Paradise*
http://www.videoparadise.com/
Video Paradise is a division of WH Smith, where you can buy videos at discounts online. All videos are in PAL format and all DVDs are region 2 coded. The site has fully secure online credit card processing. The catalogue covers action and adventure, adult interest, children's, comedy, drama, feature films, horror, musicals, opera and pop, science fiction, special interest, sport, subtitled items, thrillers, TV advertised, and wide screen items. The site has details of some special offers, and you can even find out about working for them.

*VideoZone*
http://www.videozone.co.uk
Operated from Halifax in Yorkshire, VideoZone offers a wide selection of PAL videos and laser discs. You can search through its huge database for your favourite movies, check the progress of your order, or look for new releases by your favourite stars. There is an enormous range of possible product formats. You can click to download its stock sales list, including as a zipped Word document or text file. To protect your payment card details over the internet, VideoZone use a secure web server (available for browsers that support https – which includes current versions of Microsoft Internet Explorer and Netscape). Its phone and fax numbers and postal address are shown.

## Computer games

*Entertainment Express*
http://www.entexpress.com
Entertainment Express is a creation of the retailing giant Kingfisher plc, which owns Comet, Superdrug, Woolworths and other retail chains. It has been set up to sell CDs, videos and multimedia products direct to customers who want to shop on the internet. The bright and breezy looking site includes best sellers, special offers, promotions and hot deals, new releases and advance information. It offers a big range of popular entertainment products, with free delivery in the UK, and supports all the leading console games such as PlayStation, Nintendo 64, GameBoy, and Dreamcast.

*Gameplay*
http://www.gameplay.com/
Gameplay is probably Europe's largest online games destination. Its

home page is packed with links and icons to help you shop for games, read about games and most importantly play games online. Its online shop stocks more than 3,000 lines. Gameplay says it has the world's largest games server setup with over 70 dedicated machines to keep everything running smoothly. Its friendly online community means you can meet like-minded people to chat about games and anything else.

Fig. 44. The Gameplay web site is a must for the dedicated computer games enthusiast.

*Gamezone*
http://www.thegamezone.co.uk
Gamezone offers PC games and leisure software online with free UK delivery. 'All products genuine UK versions. We do not sell inferior grey imports.' Then company is based in West Sussex.

*Games Console*
http://www.games-console.com/
This is a retail outlet for Sega, Sony, Nintendo, Gameboy and similar products. The contact details show that the company is based in Fleet, Hampshire, UK. As to VAT they say: 'For orders made from the UK or the European Union, 17.5 per cent VAT is added. All other orders are VAT free and you should click the exempt button to reduce VAT to zero.'

*Games Domain*
http://www.gamesdomain.co.uk/
The site has links to shareware, freeware, demos, FAQs, walkthroughs,

charts and general cheats. You will also find information about games programming, magazines, competitions, and more.

*Games Paradise*
http://www.GamesParadise.com/
Oxford-based Games Paradise is a division of the high street retailer, WH Smith. The site features the top title listings. You can do a quick search or full search of their online catalogue. The site uses the latest Microsoft security software to encrypt information passing between your terminal and their server. You can check the status of your order at any time, and amend your account details using your own personal password. If you are worried about your order, it is reassuring to know that you can email various named members of their customer support team.

*Games Workshop*
http://www.games-workshop.com
To enter the world of games, click one of the following categories: games workshop tour, online store, news and information, where to find games, or mail order. There are special offers on boxed sets (prices are in US dollars). You can also buy a range of handcrafted resin figures and models of characters who appear in war games. For gaming surfers there is information about job opportunities in the US. Sign up for the monthly *Games Workshop* newsletter to news of upcoming events, reports from around the world, new release sneak peeks, a question and answer section, and contests.

*Jungle.com*
http://www.jungle.com
Identifiable by its yellow and green cartoon snake, Jungle.com is a fully secure online retailer of computers (Jungle Computers), videos (Jungle Vision), games (Jungle Play), and music (Jungle Beat). If you are looking for Tomb Raider, Urban Chaos, Final Fantasy, Crazy Taxi and similar titles, this is a good place to look. It supports Dreamcast, GameBoy, Play Station, PC games and other popular games formats. The service comes complete with online order tracking. The inspiration for jungle.com came from 33-year-old founder Steve Bennett, who is also boss of one of the UK's largest computer retail and mail order companies, Software Warehouse plc, whose sales now top £100m.

*Net Megastore*
http://www.net-megastore.co.uk
Birmingham-based Net Megastore offers music, books, videos, and computer games. It supports Sony PlayStation, Sega Megadrive, Super NES, PC CD, Dreamcast, Sega GameGear, Amiga, BM 3.5" disk, Nintendo Ultra 64, Sega Saturn, Mac/PC CD, PC DVD, Sega Megadrive 32X, Sega Mega CD, PC Budget CD, and Apple Mac. The site employs the latest internet security and encryption for credit card and order processing.

*Simply Games*

http://www.simplygames.com/

Based in Clapham, London, Simply Games was set up in December 1998 as an alternative UK source for PC and console games. You can explore its range of products by clicking on little blue dropdown menus for each games format, PC, Dreamcast, Gameboy and so on. The pages contain some useful advice section for games newbies. All of its online transactions use SSL (secure socket layer) technology.

*Software Warehouse*

http://www.software-warehouse.com

This is the virtual store of Software Warehouse whose prices are around 40 per cent below the recommended retail price. Order goods from here and you will receive the option of free delivery on all UK internet orders and two free gifts. To find a product you can use text search or select a particular option (games and consoles, peripherals etc), sub range (Dreamcast, Gameboy, Playstation etc), sub category (all categories or sports only) or manufacturer and publisher (Acer, Autodesk, Borland, Busby). You can sign up here for a free internet service and get loyalty points and unlimited email addresses.

*UK Games Exchange*

http://www.ukgamesxchange.co.uk/

At UK Games Exchange you can swap your games on the internet. Whatever type of hardware you have, the site says it has other games players who want to swap their games for yours. They say: 'We will try our best to match you to someone nearby so you can swap your games. For this we charge a flat rate of £5, payable only when you agree to the swap. We also sell secondhand Playstation and Nintendo 64 games at very competitive

Fig. 45. If you want to save both time and money, Videogameseeker is well worth a visit, because it offers a free price comparison service specialising in videos.

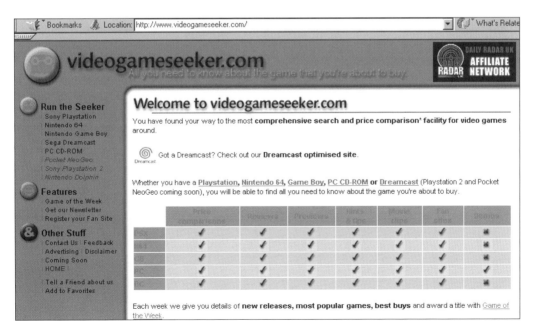

prices. We will also pay top prices for your secondhand Playstation and Nintendo 64 games from you.'

*Videogameseeker*
http://www.videogameseeker.com/
Videogameseeker is well worth checking out, if you want to be as sure as possible that you are getting the best price and delivery terms for a particular video game. It enables comparison shopping for video games sold by online stores within the UK (see chapter 3 for more about comparison shopping agents or 'bots'). You can also sign up for its newsletter about the best deals and latest releases.

## Children's toys

*British Toy & Hobby Association*
http://www.btha.co.uk/
This is the trade association of the industry which is worth around £1.6 billion per annum. It was founded in 1944 to represent the interests of UK toy manufacturers and to raise the standard of practice within the industry. It has about 220 members who between them account for 95 per cent of the British market for toys and games. You can get a good feel for the association and its membership by reading their past press releases.

*Canterbury Collectibles*
http://www.toymart.com
Canterbury Collectibles are dealers in old and collectible toys, transport, and TV related items, and have all kinds of items such as Dinky, Corgi, Matchbox, prints, art, aviation, and models. This is an excellent site. The delightful photographs make it a little slow to download, but the photos are of course vital.

*Dolls House World*
http://www.dollshouseworld.com
Dolls House World is intended for collectors and miniatures enthusiasts alike. They say: 'Every week we bring you fascinating features about dolls houses and miniaturesand the people who make and collect them. We also bring you the best of the new products, and highlight old favourites you might have missed. And best of all you can buy all of these miniature treasures online.'

*Funstore*
http://www.funstore.co.uk
This is an online toy and game store. The toys are shown in the form of lists, and you just click on the item you want to view and picture, and ordering information. Online credit card security is provided through Barclays Merchant Services and NetBanx, the UK's leading credit clearing company. You can check through the company's trading terms and conditions, which are set out in some detail.

Fig. 46. Funstore offers something for all interests and age groups. The site is very easy to navigate.

## Hamleys
http://www.hamleys.co.uk
Hamleys of Regent Street, London, is one of the world's oldest and most popular toy stores. To navigate the web site, either click a lift button to go to the floor of your choice or click the Personal Shopper. The lift buttons take you to the foyer (home page), boys' toys, creative play and puzzles, games, computer games, preschool, soft toys and girls' toys and dolls. Each floor has photos of selected toys with a brief description and price. Soft toys include Barney and Orange Fuzzy. Preschoolers will like Mr Potato Head and the dolls. Despite the many graphics the site downloads quickly.

## House of Toys
http://www.houseoftoys.com
This is a great place for antique and collectible toys including battery-operated and wind-up toys, robots, space toys, dolls, action figures, cars, and tin prints. It is a veritable online Aladdin's cave, a children's toy edition of *The Antiques Roadshow*. You will need to be patient while the images to download, but with a site like this these are essential.

## Internet Gift Store
http://www.internetgiftstore.com/
This one offers television and movie toys as well as stuffed animals. It is a good site, full of the sort of toys that adults buy for their children and for themselves. In the late 1970s, when *Star Wars* erupted onto the screen, a Super 8 short film was available in shops. This is now changing hands for hundreds of pounds. In the same way, the Beanie Babies may become collector's pieces in years to come, who knows. In the meantime you can have lots of fun wandering around this excellent store.

# Music, videos, games and toys......................................

**QUICK FIND** ⊙

**LEGO FINDER**

*Lego Group*
http://www.lego.com/
Lego has made it into cyberspace, but at the moment if you want to buy you have to be Stateside. The good thing about Lego is that it combines fun with a serious side in that it helps youngsters learn.

*Letterbox*
http://www.l-box.co.uk/
This is superb. Letterbox is a mail order company of creative and unique toys for children of all ages, located in Cornwall, UK. This is a great example of how using the internet can overcome any problem of geographical location. The site is bright and colourful looking, and downloads quickly. If you fancy a trip down memory lane, have a look at their traditional gifts.

*Schwarz*
http://www.faoschwarz.com/
Schwarz is the famous old-established American toy store, with a wonderful shop in Manhattan, New York. It is not always clear from the site whether the dolls are for children or collectors. They have one named Gene Marshall listed as a collector's doll, but then say she is suitable for children of age 7 or upwards. So perhaps it is for people of all ages. The one thing we were not too keen on, is the scenario where Gene is said to have been mistaken for a famous movie star, the dilemma is should she reveal who she really is, and 'risk losing Mr Right'?

*Tamagotchi in the UK*
http://www.ridhughz.demon.co.uk/tamagotchi/
Love them or hate them, says the site, Tamagotchi are cuteness on a keychain. The Tamagotchi is a virtual pet you can take almost anywhere. Invariably you have to, because they don't switch off like a computer; they stay on 24 hours a day, seven days a week, and sleep at night. The owner of this site is not a retailer of Tamagotchis. He simply likes the things and has set up this web site to tell the world about it. Children have been known to need bereavement counselling when one of these things 'died' when left unattended.

*Teddy Bear of Europe*
http://www.teddybears.com
This delightful retail site is a wonderful homage to teddy bears. You can find out just about everything there is to know by following the many links here – teddy bear artists, teddy bear retailers, teddy bear manufactures, teddy bear museums, teddy bear magazines and teddy bear clubs and associations of all kinds.

*Toys "Я" Us*
http://www.toysrus.co.uk
This is the company that reversed the R in its name and made a hit on both sides of the Atlantic. The UK-based online shop includes a 'nearest store' feature. From time to time the site offers special internet prices where the product is highlighted with a special flag. Toys R Us uses

encryption techniques – secure socket layer (SSL) technology – to ensure that your credit card details are safely processed. They aim to deliver your order within three working days. The site also has links to some of the top toy sites on the internet.

Fig. 47. The home page of Toys R Us, which offers a home delivery service, and free links to some of the top toy sites on the world wide web.

# 7 Books, newspapers and magazines

**In this chapter we will explore:**

▶ *online bookstores*

▶ *book price comparison web sites*

▶ *secondhand and antiquarian booksellers*

▶ *online news and magazine links*

▶ *UK national newspapers*

This chapter brings you links to some of the world's best web sites for reading matter. All the top book bookstores, newspapers and magazines now have their own web sites, which you can generally access free. Books were among the first products to be sold successfully across the internet, and the online bookseller Amazon became the top retailing site on the net.

Many news and magazine publishers have huge online archives of articles and features from previous editions, which you can explore (usually requiring free registration). An increasing number of sites seem to want not just customers but 'members', in order to extract as much personal data about people as possible.

Fig. 48. Amazon was the first internet retailer to gain worldwide recognition. Its main offering was books, but it has now expanded into many other products and services, capitalising on its well-established brand name.

## Online bookstores

*Alphabetstreet Books*
http://www.alphabetstreet.com
This is one of the leading UK online bookstores, started in 1996 and backed by FreeServe. Free 'informers' can be sent to you by email every two weeks or so, to keep you up to date on hundreds of subjects. You can

search and browse for any book, and order using their secure internet credit and debit card payment system. The service is part of Streets On-line. Its other online retailing sites sell CDs, DVDs and games. Most of its products include VAT and free delivery in the UK.

*Amazon*
http://www.amazon.com
Founded by entrepreneur Jeff Bezos, Amazon opened its virtual doors in 1995 with a mission to transform book-buying into the fastest, easiest, and most enjoyable shopping experience possible. Since then more than 12 million people in more than 160 countries have used it – not just for books but for electronic greeting cards, online auctions, CDs, videos, DVDs, toys and games, and electronics. Whatever your interest in books, this site is unmissable. Amazon is one of the top 10 web sites on the planet. It has a dedicated UK site at: http://www.amazon.co.uk

*Barnes and Noble*
http://www.barnesandnoble.com
Barnes & Noble is one of the top US retail bookstore chains, and this in-depth site reflects the company's dominant position in the marketplace. You can search for what you want and browse in all sorts of ways for example by subject – biography, business, computers, entertainment, fiction, literature, kids' books, history, mind, body, and spirit and many more subjects. Since launching in 1997, this has become the world's fifth largest ecommerce site and among the 25 largest sites overall on the web, according to Media Metrix. It is also the exclusive bookseller on America Online.

*Blackwells*
http://bookshop.blackwell.co.uk/
Based in Oxford, the 'world's leading academic bookseller' would like you to be not just a customer but a member. Registration is free and brings an email, alerting service, a one-time entry of up to four delivery addresses, a personalised notebook and diary, order history and profile and a perso-nalised homepage. But it's not essential for using the site. Blackwell's Online Bookshop offers free postage on orders to UK addresses.

*BOL*
http://www.bol.com
BOL is a heavyweight contender in the online bookselling market, offer-ing dedicated services for the UK, USA, Germany, France, the Netherlands, Spain and Switzerland. You can choose to create your own profile, tailoring the service to suit your individual requirements. You will then receive personalised book recommendations and news. You can easily check the status of your order. BOL is a division of the media giant Bertlesmann.

*Book Pl@ce*
http://www.thebookplace.com
Bookpl@ce is another UK challenger in the fiercely competitive market for online bookselling. The site includes nearly a billion items indexed for

searching, including titles and author names. Book blurbs and jackets are shown in many cases. It also offers *Book Ends,* a free online magazine, and Fifth Dimension, its own sci-fi and fantasy bookshop. The service is owned and operated by Book Data in London. Any non-stock item has to be ordered from the publishers, so delivery could take 14 days.

*Book Search Engine*
http://www.booksearchengine.com
If it is in print, you should be able find the cheapest and nearest copy here. You don't need to type in the author's full name or the complete title in most cases. For example, if searching for *The Power and the Glory* by Graham Greene, you could just type in Greene in the author field and Glory in the title field.

Fig. 49. Booksearchengine is a must for the book collector, or for any book buyer who needs to save time as well as money online.

Fig. 50. Bookwebsites is a major portal site for the world of books, newspaper and magazines. If you can't find it here, it probably doesn't exist.

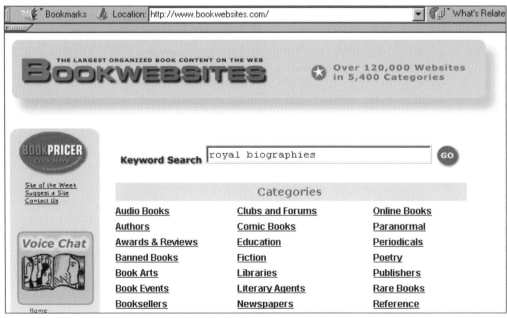

*Book Web Sites*
http://www.bookwebsites.com/
Run from Los Angeles, this is an outstandingly functional and useful resource for booklovers. It contains links to a whopping 120,000 web sites
in more than 5,000 different categories. Highly recommended.

*Borders*
http://www.borders.com
The Borders Group of the USA is the world's second largest retailer of
books, music, video and other informational, educational, and entertainment products. It has over 200 superstores in the USA, UK and
Singapore. If it's a new or in-print product you want, then with a searchable and browsable catalogue of ten million books, CDs and videos, you
should find it on this fast-loading site.

Fig. 51. The web site of
Borders, one of the
world's biggest chain of
book retailers. It includes
an order-tracking facility
for its online customers.

*Computer Manuals Online Bookstore*
http://www.compman.co.uk/home.htm
This attractively presented UK site should be able to supply almost any
kind of computer manual or reference book you could want.

*Fred Hanna's Bookstore*
http://www.adnet.ie/hannas/
Hanna is one of the top bookselling names in Ireland. In addition to comprehensive online searching and ordering facilities, the site also contains
links to other Irish web sites of interest.

# Books, newspapers and magazines.....................................

*Heffers*

http://www.heffers.co.uk

Cambridge-based Heffers offers secure online shopping on this functional site, with use of a login name and password. Its database lists around 1.9 million titles. If the title you want is out of print or secondhand you can make use of its antiquarian and out-of-print books search. As a 'member', you can sign on to receive information on new books in any of over 3,400 subject categories. Heffers is now part of Blackwell.

*Helter Skelter*

http://www.skelter.demon.co.uk

Based in London's West End, Helter Skelter claims to be the only rock 'n' roll bookshop in the world, and able to get any music book available anywhere in the world to anywhere in the world. You can download its current catalogue in MS Word format.

*Hodges Figgis*

http://www.hodgesfiggis.com

Hodges Figgis is a top bookseller in Ireland. To find a specific title on its online store you are invited to browse or search its catalogue of over 100,000 titles. You choose the subject category you want, and then further options are presented to you. Alternatively, you can key in a title, author or ISBN. If you cannot find the book you are looking for on the site, you can an email them and they will try and help you.

*Internet Bookshop*

http://www.bookshop.co.uk/

Originally an independent internet start up business, the Internet Bookshop has been acquired by WH Smith, the high street retailer, and rebranded as WHSmith Online. This attractive site offers well over a million titles in all subject areas, many of them discounted. The site is well presented in a magazine-style format, with news, reviews and features. It also sells CDs, videos and games. It uses a secure credit card ordering system. Recommended.

*Ottakars*

http://www.ottakars.com/

Ottakars was set up in 1987, and now has about 70 bookshops across the UK. Its attractively produced online bookstore offers a 30-day satisfaction guarantee. You can search by author, title, ISBN or keywords, or browse by various subject categories. Each branch offers its own highly individual web site.

*Read Ireland*

http://www.readireland.ie

Based in Dublin, Read Ireland is an internet bookstore dedicated exclusively to Irish interest books. It offers a free weekly email newsletter.

*Scotweb*
http://www.scotweb.co.uk/library/
Scotweb features a selection of Scottish books and magazines, Robert Burns and other literature, and multimedia CDs about Scotland.

*John Smith & Son*
http://www.johnsmith.co.uk
Founded in Glasgow in 1751, John Smith is Scotland's oldest independent book retailer, and believes it may be the oldest continuously trading bookseller in the world. It has twelve shops in Scotland, eight of them on university campuses. They say that every hundredth order received from this web site is supplied free of charge.

*W H Smith*
See the Internet Bookshop (above).

*James Thin*
http://www.jthin.co.uk/
Established in 1848, Thin's are famous Scottish and international booksellers. Their site offers a quick search facility through a database of around one million titles. It also features details of forthcoming events, signings and readings, and *Capital Letters*, an online magazine featuring news and reviews from the Scottish literary world.

*Waterstones*
http://www.waterstones.co.uk/
With its attractive presentation, quick search, links to branches, personal library, music, and numerous other features, Waterstones has developed an impressive and functional site. You can take a site tour, explore current title and author promotions, books of the month, signed first editions, out-of-print titles and check out discounts on best-selling titles. You can track your online order using a case-sensitive username and password.

▶ *Finding out more* – For a more detailed coverage of the huge online world of books, authors, libraries and writing, see *Books and Publishing on the Internet* (Internet Handbooks).

## Book price comparison web sites

*Deal Time*
http://www.dealtime.com/
You can use Deal Time to find almost any book, CD, video or DVD on the internet and then let it compare prices from all major online shops to track down the best offer. You are also invited to enhance your web site, increase your traffic and earn money by joining the Deal Time partner program. Highly recommended.

*AddAll*
http://www.addall.com/
AddAll is a free and independent web site and search engine built by

book buyers for book buyers. They say: 'Our search result is totally objective without favouring one bookstore over another.' You can search for any book you want, and compare the prices, from around 40 online bookstores worldwide. You can have the prices displayed in the currency you prefer, along with the delivery charge and any sales tax applicable to your region. You can also compare delivery times.

*A1-BookMall*
http://www.a1bookmall.com/

A1-BookMall is another very effective book-price search engine. You can compare the prices of 25 internet bookstores, and the shipping costs are displayed in the comparison

Fig. 52. A1Bookmall is a first class book price comparison search engine.

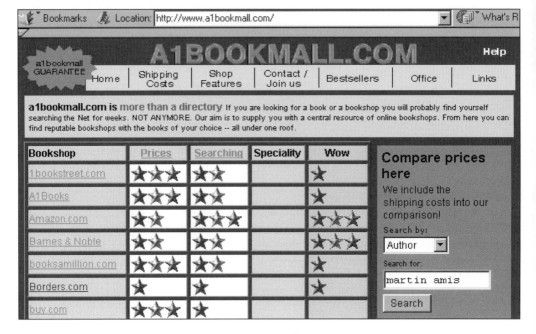

*Best Book Buys*
http://www.bestbookbuys.com/
This one finds the lowest price from several online bookstores including Amazon, Barnes & Noble, Big Words, Book Pool, BooksaMillion, Buy.-Com, Christian Book, Fat Brain, Page One, Powell's Books, Textbooks, Varsity Books and many more. There is an associated web site called Best Music Buys.

## Rare and secondhand online booksellers

*Advanced Book Exchange*
http://www.abebooks.com
The Canadian company ABE is probably the world's largest source of out-of-print books. It represents the stocks of over 5,300 booksellers, with 15 million individual titles listed. ABE networks with thousands of bookstores, most of them small family businesses who could have that

scarce book you want. Do you want a copy of that elusive first edition, or the long-ago published memoirs of your great-grandfather? ABE is the place to come. Highly recommended.

*Bibliofind*
http://bibliofind.com/
With more than ten million used and rare books, first editions, periodicals and ephemera offered for sale by thousands of booksellers around the world, Bibliofind is one of the most interesting secondhand book-selling sites on the web, and a must for collectors and dealers worldwide. The functionally laid out site displays the answers to your questions in seconds. Bibliofind has recently become part of the mighty Amazon group of online retailing services. Highly recommended.

*Bookfinder.com*
http://www.bookfinder.com
'Over 15 million new, used, rare, and out of print books at your fingertips...' BookFinder connects readers to over 15,000 booksellers from around the world with a real open marketplace for all their online book shopping needs. You can use this handy site to search ABE, Amazon Bibliofind, Bibliocity, BookAvenue, Antiqbook and other online stores.

*British Internet Bookdealers Association*
http://www.clique.co.uk/bibfind.htm
The site contains details of more than 1,300 British book dealers and their specialist subject-areas. There is a search engine where you can seek information by keying in a subject area, otherwise you will need to know the name of particular dealer you are looking for.

*Charing Cross Road Bookshop*
http://www.anyamountofbooks.com/
These two London shops – Charing Cross Road Bookshop and Any Amount of Books – can supply rare books, first editions, modern literature, art, poetry, scholarly/academic books, antiquarian, leather bound sets, and general stock. The site contains their catalogue, plus some useful links to the secondhand book trade.

*Provincial Booksellers Fairs Association*
http://antiquarian.com/pbfa/
The PBFA is the largest trade association in the world for dealers in antiquarian and secondhand books, well known for the 150 book fairs it organises each year around the UK. The site includes a directory of members, notice board, and details and dates of fairs. The annual highlight is the series of fairs held in May/June at the Russell Hotel in Bloomsbury, London.

## Online news and magazine links

*All Newspapers*
http://www.allnewspapers.com
The site offers links to top stories and to local, national, and international newspapers, magazines, electronic media, and news agencies.

**Welcome to**
**bibliofind**

Nine million used, antiquarian and rare books, periodicals and ephemera offered for sale by thousands of booksellers around the world make this the largest and most interesting bookselling site on the Web.

# Books, newspapers and magazines......................................

*Book Web Sites*
http://www.bookwebsites.com/
Despite its name, this site has a huge and very clearly organised set of links to newspapers all over the world, organised by continent and then by country. On the home page, click the link to Newspapers or Periodicals. There are thousands of links, though the coverage is patchy in places. Recommended.

*E&P Directory of Online Newspapers*
http://www.mediainfo.com/emedia/
Do you fancy reading *Le Soir*, *The Miami Herald*, *The Wall Street Journal* or *Asia Times*? This is a substantial database of newspapers all over the world, complete with an easy-to-use search function. It is run by *Editor & Publisher*, a 116-year-old magazine covering the newspaper industry in North America.

*Ecola's Newsstand: Magazines*
http://www.ecola.com/news/magazine/
This is an easy-to-use and searchable guide to over 500 magazines which have their own updated web sites.

*Electronic Newsstand*
http://home.worldonline.dk/~knud-sor/en/
Run by a Dane, this enterprising site contains links to the web sites of newspapers all over the world. The home page leads to a clickable world map, where you click on a region of he world for which you want more detailed information. The site offers subscriptions for more than 850 magazines as well as recommendations, media commentary, community discussions, and fresh content daily.

Fig. 53. The Electronic Newsstand offers handy links to all kinds of media-related web sites, from traditional newspapers and magazines to online weather reports, newsletters and e-zines.

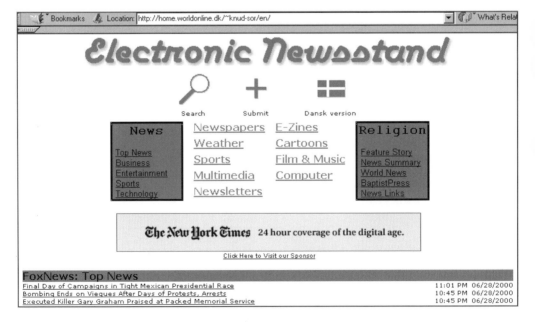

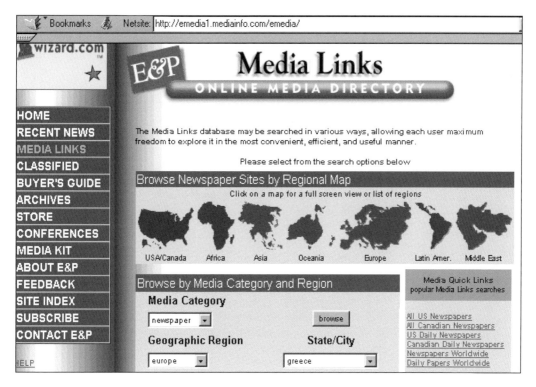

*Magazine Rack*
http://www.magazine-rack.com
Here are all the magazines you care to read, all online and all free. There are hundreds of titles available, and a search facility to help you.

*NewsBot*
http://www.newsbot.com/
You can use NewsBot as your 'news-agent', specifying a topic and a time frame. The bot will then go off to search and clip articles from many sources, and display the results in your browser window.

*NewsDirectory*
http://www.newsdirectory.com/
This is a fantastic guide to English-language media online. It contains categorised information links to more than 17,000 newspaper and magazine titles all over the world. If you are more interested in subject matter than the name of the newspaper, there is a feature called the Electric Library, where you can do a keyword search of millions of articles.

*News Index*
http://www.newsindex.com/
Founded in April 1996, News Index is a searchable index of the latest news articles published on the web. News Index indexes current articles only: it is not an archive. They say: 'Despite what every news outlet wants you to believe, no single outlet delivers the truth, they all deliver their

Fig. 54. E&P Media Links is an outstanding portal site for worldwide media. You can search for what you want by media category, geographic region, or subjectmatter.

version of the story Only through reading many different versions of a story, can you finally derive some semblance of what actually occurred.'

*Newsrack*
http://www.newsrack.com/
Here you will find a good collection of the online versions of newspapers and magazines from around the world. Access to the site is slowed down by some rather distracting animated graphics.

*NewsTrawler*
http://www.newstrawler.com/
NewsTrawler is a 'parallel search engine' for news on the Internet. You can search for articles from the archives of literally hundreds of online news, magazine and journal sources from around the world. You can personalise your NewsTrawler search preferences in various ways.

Fig. 55. The Paperboy offers a simple no-nonsense gateway to newspapers everywhere. For example here, on the left, it has links to all the top newspapers in Canada.

*Paper Boy*
http://www.thepaperboy.com
Run by an enterprising former law student in Australia, Paperboy is another site that offers a quick and convenient way to access newspapers and magazines around the world. Clicking on Singapore, for example, produced links to the web sites of 9 Singaporean newspapers and magazines.

*PubList*
http://www.publist.com
PubList is an interet-based guide to more than 150,000 domestic and international print and electronic publications including magazines, journals, e-journals, newsletters, and monographs. It provides quick and easy access to titles, formats, publisher addresses, editor contacts, circulation data, and ISSN numbers. It also provides access to subscription services as well as article level information through rights and permissions providers and document delivery services.

## UK newspapers

*The Daily Mail*
http://www.dailymail.co.uk
This site is the online version of the *Daily Mail*'s IT supplement, covering computers and information technology, every Tuesday in the *Daily Mail*. This site is produced by Associated New Media, creators of This Is London, the Evening Standard Online. Associated Newspapers also owns UK Plus, This is London, and SoccerNet.

*The Daily Telegraph*
http://www.telegraph.co.uk
Presented in striking conservative blue and yellow, the site offers a front page, UK and international news, weather, crosswords, and feedback (with opportunities to vote and comment on topical issues). There is city and business news, sport, a review section, travel, motoring, property, education, appointments, classifieds, and more.

*The Daily Star*
http://www.megastar.co.uk/
Against a home page of blazing red, the 'MegaStar' offers characteristically over-the-top news, sport, chat, babes and more, on a web site clearly designed to preserve traditional tabloid values. The site features a virtual reality bar (plugin required), 'laughs', Mega Posters, a shop bot, and more.

*The European*
http://www.the-european.com/
Launched in 1990, the European is an A3 magazine, published weekly on Monday. There is a predominantly male readership estimated at 600,000 worldwide. To view the electronic paper you will need Adobe Acrobat Reader 3.

*The Evening Standard: This is London*
http://www.thisislondon.co.uk

*The Express*
http://www.lineone.net/express/
The site has rather a tabloid feel, but is clearly presented and easy to navigate. It includes ITN video news, UK news, newswire, royal watch, weather, world news, plus quick links to UK papers and world papers.

# Books, newspapers and magazines.....................................

Fig. 56. The *Financial Times* newspaper has established a major online presence, some of which is available free, and some of which requires a subscription.

### The Financial Times
http://www.ft.com
The original pink pages: an authoritative source and every-growing database of information about UK and international investment and business.

### The Guardian and The Observer
http://www.guardianunlimited.co.uk
Radical and probing daily journalism on your desktop.

### The Independent
http://www.independent.co.uk
For intelligent comment and in-depth features on current national and international issues.

### Jewish Chronicle
http://www.jchron.co.uk/
The world's oldest and most influential Jewish newspaper, the London-based *Jewish Chronicle* has a 158-year history of editorial independence. It offers news and opinion, film, theatre, travel, cookery and youth and singles events.

### The Mail on Sunday
http://www.mailonsunday.co.uk
Traditional middle England and conservative family values are voiced uncompromisingly here.

### The Mirror
http://www.mirror.co.uk
The Mirror's rather downbeat home page offers links to online news,

sport, features, Matthew Wright, Miriam Stoppard, Victor Lewis Smith, and the Voice of the Mirror. Born into a tradition of questioning the status quo, *The Mirror* remains as quick as ever to challenge the establishment of the day. It's the paper that tells it like it (thinks it) is.

*The News of the World*
http://www.newsoftheworld.co.uk/
Outspoken comment on topical issues from opinionated columnists such as Richard Stott. There is an endless supply of stories about celebs, scandals, politics, and sport, plus something on motoring, movies, video, theatre, travel, holidays and business.

*The Sun*
http://www.the-sun.co.uk/
http://www.bun.com/
*The Sun* seems to have a Jekyll and Hyde personality. It has gone online with two contrasting web sites: the main Sun web site with a typical tabloid presentation, and a site called Bun, whose name derives from Cockney rhyming slang, CurrantBun. This somewhat low-key offering provides access to news headlines and stories. It can also act as your internet service provider, offering totally free internet access, unlimited email addresses, various web tools, and some online shopping.

*The Sunday Mirror*
http://www.sundaymirror.co.uk
You can follow the news and sport headlines, and other features, from this easy-to-navigate but rather dull-looking web site.

*The Sunday Times*
http://www.sunday-times.co.uk
No more struggling with all those heavy supplements, once you are on-line.

*The Times*
http://www.the-times.co.uk
The flagship of the vast Murdoch news empire.

▶ *Finding out more* – For a more detailed coverage of internet media and broadcasting web sites, see *News & Magazines on the Internet* (Internet Handbooks).

# 8 Food and drink

### In this chapter we will explore:

▶ *online food suppliers*

▶ *traditional food and grocery stores*

▶ *wines, beers and spirits*

▶ *food and wine magazines*

## Online food suppliers

*American Spoon Foods*
http://www.spoon.com/
The site has a foods catalogue, recipes and online shopping facilities. It specialises in gourmet jams, jellies, preserves, and condiments, gift baskets, and sugar-free products. Its products are sold through mail order, retail, food service, and wholesale channels.

*Ben & Jerry's Ice Cream*
http://www.benjerry.co.uk/
Quirky Vermont-based ice cream maker Ben & Jerry's has breathed new life into the UK ice cream market with its 'tubtastic' range of 'cheekily chunky, three-dimensional' ice creams. This company was started by two childhood buddies, who took on the heavyweight competition of the existing industry. Today they have a cult following and are noted for a continuing stream of nutty names and improbable flavour combinations. You can buy online from the gift shop (goody bags and ice cream vouchers).

Fig. 57. The home page of Food Connect, which describes itself as a club for lovers of fine food.

*Brits Abroad*
http://www.britsabroad.co.uk
The company delivers British food worldwide for Anglophiles and ex-pats. It stocks over 900 grocery items – cereals, spreads, baby products, sweets and crisps, teas, pickles and many others – and says it will source others on request. The web site has a secure online ordering system, and a wide range of cards is accepted.

*Chocolatestore*
http://www.chocolatestore.com/
This is a great place to come for truffles, pralines and liqueurs in dark, milk and white chocolate, mostly handmade by award-winning Belgian, Swiss and French chocolatiers. You can browse through its luxury cocoa-rich product selections, explore the recipes in its cookery section, or visit the Melting Pot area for advice and information. A typical offering is Handmade English Fruit Truffles at £12.99, offering delicious combinations of lemon and strawberry or blackcurrant and raspberry truffles, handmade in Devon specially for Chocolatestore. The site belongs to the Which? Webtrader Code of Practice. You can contact them by email, fax, phone or post.

*Definitely Devon*
http://www.definitelydevon.co.uk/
This is a co-operative of dairy farmers in north Devon selling milk, cream, and clotted cream.

*Duerr's*
http://www.duerrs.co.uk/
Based in Manchester, Duerr's is one of Britain's top jam makers, founded in 1881. Today it fills 250,000 jars every day with jams, mincemeat, marmalade and peanut butter. It has developed an imaginative web site complete with recipes, entertaining animations, sound effects, video, and a slide-show tour

*Everpure*
http://www.everpure.com/
Everpure supplies drinking water systems, water filters and water treatment products. This site is packed with information about water, and public health aspects. It discusses the bacteria that can affect water and how it can infect us. Click on the Consumer icon to find out more.

*Foodconnect*
http://www.foodconnect.co.uk
This attractively designed and useful site brings you providers of speciality foods, and offers related news and features. There are handy links to bakery, butchers, dairy, delicatessen, drinks, fishmongers, gifts, greengrocers and organics. The site's many features include a recipe selected and retail locator.

# Food and drink..........................................................

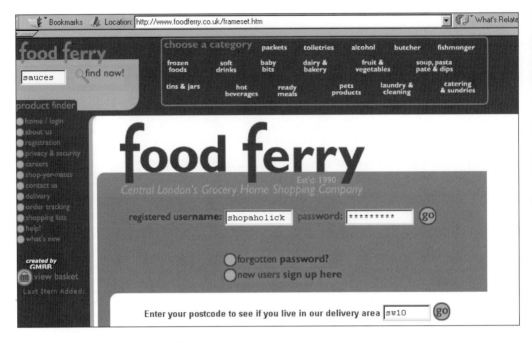

choose a category   packets   toiletries   alcohol   butcher   fishmonger

frozen foods   soft drinks   baby bits   dairy & bakery   fruit & vegetables   soup, pasta paté & dips

tins & jars   hot beverages   ready meals   pets products   laundry & cleaning   catering & sundries

sauces   find now!

food ferry

product finder

- home / login
- about us
- registration
- privacy & security
- careers
- shop-yer-mates
- contact us
- delivery
- order tracking
- shopping lists
- help!
- what's new

created by
GMRR

view basket
Last Item Added:

**food ferry**
Est'd: 1990
Central London's Grocery Home Shopping Company

registered username: shopaholick   password: **********   go

○ forgotten **password**?
○ new users **sign up here**

Enter your postcode to see if you live in our delivery area   sw10   go

Fig. 58. Food Ferry has developed an internet-based food delivery service for people living in greater London, obviating the need to fight the crowds and the traffic.

## Food Ferry
http://www.foodferry.co.uk/
Founded about ten years ago by Jonathan Hartnell-Beavis and James Millar, Food Ferry provides home delivery of groceries across central London. Its web site is packed with useful categories such as tins and jars, hot beverages, ready meals, soups, pasta, dips, butcher, fishmonger and many others. Enter your London postcode to make sure you are on one of their delivery routes.

## Food Ingredients on the Internet
http://www.fioti.com/index.htm
The free search area allows you to find companies, products and contacts from the Fioti database. You can search across different criteria, quickly and easily.

## French Hamper Company
http://www.frenchhampers.com/
The French Hamper Company is based in Aston Clinton, in Buckinghamshire. It specialises in top quality French foods and wines. The service is run by Philippe Brillant, a French chef with long experience of working in Michelin-starred restaurants, and who was a chef to the Saudi royal family. The company supplies food and wine for the social events of the year such as Ascot, Newmarket, Henley and Wimbledon. Do you lust for a hamper containing a couple of bottles of Yquem and Petrus? Look no further. The recipes are helpfully provided in both French and English. The site offers secure online transactions, and has signed up to the Which?Webtrader code of practice.

Fig. 59. Food Ingredients on the Internet (Fioti) is an excellent place to track down those elusive ingredients you need for that special occasion.

### Gourmet Guides
http://www.gourmetguides.com/
This Seattle-based business produces cookbooks for every kind of cook – professional chefs, serious cookbook collectors, and home cooks, and has been doing so since 1973. Some of its prices are discounted by 40 to 75 per cent.

### Gourmet Ireland
http://www.gourmetireland.com/
Visit this web site to explore the natural foods of Ireland. Developed by Irish TV chefs Paul and Jeanne Rankine, it provides recipes, gift hampers, news items and more.

### Gunpowder Foods
http://www.bigbruce.com/
Gunpowder Foods is dedicated to bringing you high quality gourmet spices, seasonings and mixes. Once again this is an American site, reflecting the lead of the US on the internet. Be warned, all the recipes that are listed here are for hot chilli type foods, so if you are a plain boiled beef and carrots person, this aptly-named site is probably not for you.

### Heath Mall
http://www.hlthmall.com/
Heath Mall is a natural products shopping mall of businesses specialising in health, nutrition, fitness and personal development. The health issues involved in over-eating are worth reviewing. It comes with supermarket-type background music.

### Heinz Direct
http://www.heinz.co.uk/
The Heinz Direct web site lets you order cases of your favourite Heinz products or gift hampers and have them delivered straight to your door

# Food and drink............................................................

"Hungry for Heinz but unable to find your favourite varieties locally?"

**HEINZ DIRECT**

**Enter the Store**
Choose your favourite UK Heinz products to be delivered to your door. Enter the store, and you're one click nearer to a taste of home, wherever you are.

**ENTER**

When you have finished your shopping, why not visit the Heinz UK and Ireland site at www.heinz.co.uk

If you are unable to order using this site, call +44 (0) 1379 649646.

**W**elcome To Heinz Direct, you can order your favourite Heinz products on the World Wide Web for despatch to almost anywhere in the world.

TRADE USER   If you are interested in Heinz Trade or Foodservice, click here

NEW USER   If you are new to Heinz Direct, click here

Our online store is packed with your favourite Heinz groceries, pickles and sauces, as well as Heinz baby and Farley's baby foods. We have also put together two very special gift hampers.

Our Grocery Gift Hamper is designed to meet the needs of those who are longing for the taste of home, while our Baby Gift Hamper is the ideal gift for mum and mums-to-be.

About this Service

Order Status

Feedback

Help

Fig. 60. Heinz is one of many food manufacturers with an online presence, and this one is open to the public as well as to people in the food business.

– anywhere in the world. You can order them for yourself or send them as a present to a relative or friend. Just choose from categories such as sauces and pickles and Farley's baby food. You can then select a specific product, destination and choose between standard and express delivery. You can add a message if you are sending a gift hamper.

*Jane Asher Party Cakes*
http://www.jane-asher.co.uk/
This is the culinary web site of the television presenter, cook, author and former model who once dressed in a chocolate dress for an advertising feature. Jane Asher's real-life cake shop and tearoom is in Chelsea, London. She has another site on sugarcraft, to which there is a link here. If you are interested in quality foods and creating spectacular decorative effects, this is certainly worth a visit.

*Jewish Food Guide*
http://www.kosher.org.uk/guide.html
The site opens with a message from Rabbi Conway discussing *The Really Jewish Food Guide*, a published book you can obtain from here. You can be kept up to date by email.

*Kelloggs UK*
http://www.kelloggs.co.uk/
A new UK Kellogg's web site shop is in preparation. They say: 'Here you will be able to get your hands on some great Kellogg's merchandise, with perfect gifts for all the family at fantastic, low prices – without the need for tokens.' Meantime the site contains food facts, news, competitions, recipes and links to sister sites.

## Kitchen Link

http://www.kitchenlink.com/

The US site Kitchen Link describes itself as 'your guide to what's cooking the net.' It contains a staggering index of more than 10,000 food and cookery links on the net. Its many features include discussion boards, a cookery club, recipes and restaurant menus, health issues, hot topics and more. The site is well worth exploring for these efficiently organised links alone.

Fig. 61. Kitchen Link is a wonderful gateway site leading to a huge number of food and cookery links all over the world wide web. It includes message boards so you can swap information and tips with fellow cooks.

## Macdonald's Smoked Gourmet Foods

http://www.smokedproduce.co.uk/macdonalds/index.htm

This Scottish Highlands firm offers an appetising range of smoked salmon, game, cheeses, haggis, heather tea, venison and – rather surprisingly – alligator.

## Meat Matters

http://www.meatmatters.com/

This is a site for the hard-pressed British meat industry, with suggested menus and recipes, and information about beef, lamb and pork.

## Middle England Fine Foods

http://www.meff.co.uk/

Launched in 1996, MEFF is a regional association for producers and processors of speciality food and drink in the East Midlands, in particular Derbyshire, Leicestershire, Lincolnshire, Northamptonshire, and Nottinghamshire. The icons (which could be better labelled) include categories such as bakery, dairy, fish, fresh produce, meat, poultry, game, preserves, prepared foods, honey, and several others. Clicking on these takes you to descriptive lists of suppliers, with their email and web site addresses.

# Food and drink.....

*Muslim Food Board*

http://www.halaal.demon.co.uk/mfbintro.htm

The UK Muslim Food Board was formed in 1992 as an independent, non-profit making organisation serving halaal consumers throughout UK. It has a number of consultancy roles. It gives expert advice on halaal food in accordance to the dietary laws of Islam. It undertakes detailed investigation into the availability of food products, and determines their suitability for halaal consumption. It then publishes its findings.

*Neuchatel Chocolates*

http://www.neuchatelchocolates.com/

This is a site that a chocaholic might die for. Swiss chocolate is among the finest in the world and this site is dedicated to preserving that tradition. We loved the information on chocolate truffles – impossible to read without drooling. Even if you do not buy, you can enjoy the vicarious pleasure of seeing how a craftsman creates hand-made chocolates.

*New York City Gourmet Food*

http://www.nycfood.com/

Here you can explore one of New York's oldest and most famous restaurants and delicatessens. One of the great bonuses of American cultural diversity is the enormous range of food styles that are available.

*North West Fine Foods*

http://www.nw-fine-foods.co.uk/

This is a guide to speciality food and drink producers in the north-west of the UK. You'll find the usual links to bakery, beverages, dairy products, preserves and the like. For example, the link to prepared foods led to specialist curries, lasagnes, boeuf bourgignon, delicatessen salads and fresh chilled curry sauces. The site incorporates a speciality British food search facility.

*Nutrition Now*

http://www.nutritionnow.com/

Nutrition Now site offers natural vitamins and herbal supplements for men, women, children and pets. Free brochures are available. The firm has been in business for over 17 years. This is an excellent site showing what can be done in terms of niche marketing. They will deliver, but if you buy over the internet you should remember to check out their minimum order value. Their products may be subject to import restrictions or taxes, so check with the Customs and Excise before you buy.

*Organics Direct*

http://www.organicsdirect.co.uk/

This London company supplies organic food, beverages and clothing, and will deliver to your door anywhere on the UK mainland. They say: 'Choose from a huge range including fresh fruit and vegetables, dairy produce, hand-made breads, items for the store cupboard, award-winning wines, beers, Baby Organix products, and even organic clothes and nappies!' Credit card details are processed through a secure server.

*Raisin Rack*
http://www.raisinrack.com/
Raisin Rack is a dedicated natural food store featuring vitamins, minerals, herbs, groceries, organic produce and skin-care products at competitive prices.

*Real Food Market*
http://www.real-food.co.uk/
RFM offers real and organic food from a variety of smaller and independent suppliers for purchase online. They say: 'Real Food is organic pork produced from free range pigs; it's smoked mackerel from a smoke house in Cornwall; it's creamy Caerphilly cheese, hand-made in the Welsh hills'. It is also a database-driven web site allowing you to browse the market, adding products to your virtual shopping basket from as many of the traders as you like. You can then pay by credit card with the benefit of their secure server and Verisign Digital certificate.

*Riverside Foods*
http://www.riverside-smoked-foods.co.uk/
Located in Cockermouth in the Lake District, Riverside Foods is a traditional family firm of smokers and suppliers. It can supply smoked fish, meat, poultry, cheese and sausage products delivered to your door.

*Scottish Food and Drink*
http://www.scottishfoodanddrink.com
Here you will find links to more than 1,500 Scottish food and drink producers, and food advisers.

*Taste of the South East*
http://www.taste-ofthe-southeast.co.uk/
This is a useful guide to speciality food and drink producers in Surrey, East Sussex and West Sussex. This site has been designed for easy location of products by food category. Just click on the link on the left of the screen to view the members' details including their email and web site addresses. For example the section on meat, poultry and game led to everything from Horsham bacon and pork, to chicken and duck sausages, and even ostrich meat.

*UK Restaurants Directory*
http://www.restaurants.co.uk/
This is an excellent portal site to UK restaurants. A drop down menu enables you to search for restaurants of all kinds in every part of the UK. You'll find British steak houses, traditional cafés, pubs, carveries, Indian curry and balti houses, Italian pizzeria and trattoria, French bistros and brasseries, vegetarian restaurants, Japanese restaurants, cafés and takeaways. The professionally produced site also contains recipes, catering supplies, reviews, links, and updates.

# Food and drink........................................................

## Traditional food and grocery stores

### Aldi UK
http://www.aldi-stores.co.uk/
Aldi is one of the world's leading grocery retailers. Its first stores opened in the Ruhr Valley in Germany over 40 years ago and today it has thousands of stores throughout Europe, the USA and the UK. When reviewed it did not yet offer online shopping in the UK. A clickable map shows its 250 UK store locations.

### Asda
http://www.asda.co.uk/
This is the web site of the company whose name is derived from Associated Dairies. Today it is a leading chain of UK grocery stores owned by the American retail giant Walmart. The site includes a store locator, and various product and special offers and other features, but online shopping did not appear to be available when we reviewed it.

### Budgens
http://www.budgens.com/
Budgens is a UK chain of around 200 food stores. The web site offers an online store locator, and details of its service Budgens Direct. For this, you click on the items that you want on screen. Everything is then picked, securely packed and delivered to you next day. When reviewed, Budgens was offering free delivery on orders over £50, and a £5 voucher with your first order over £50

### Fortnum & Mason
http://fortnumandmason.co.uk
This famous London Piccadilly store has been supplying gourmet and quality goods to the world since 1707. If you are shopping for a special gift, or just want to treat yourself, this is one of the best sites of its kind.

### Iceland Frozen Foods
http://www.iceland.co.uk
This is the excellent site of the UK high street frozen foods supermarket. You can order online for delivery to your door, with 97 per cent of the UK now covered. You will need to register as a new customer, after which you can save your login details (username and password) on your computer. You can customise your online shopping cart for repeat orders. Your order will be electronically transmitted to your nearest store, where staff pick and pack the shopping. This is then delivered in a refrigerated van the next day. You can select a delivery slot within a two-hour period, normally between 10am and 8pm. Earlier and later slots are available at some stores. You can also shop by phone, using a catalogue called Talking Food, which they will send you.

**Iceland**.co.uk

HOME
SHOP NOW
3 WAYS TO SHOP
FOOD YOU CAN TRUST
MEAL IDEAS AND DEALS
STORE FINDER
APPLIANCES
JOBS
OUR COMPANY
JOURNALISTS
INVESTOR RELATIONS
CONTACT US
SEARCH

### Safeway
http://www.safeway.co.uk
This is the home page of the UK high street grocery chain. Reviewing

web sites can mean wading through dross at times, and to see well-designed pages is a relief. We were pleased to find a shopping list – at last online supermarket shopping UK style? No such luck, on the day we visited this was simply a device to use before you trekked down to the local high street or out of town version. At the time of writing they were testing new techniques in various branches but these involved visiting the store.

*Sainsbury's*
http://www.sainsburys.co.uk/
Sainsbury's is one of the UK's top grocery superstores and a keen rival of Tesco. In late 2000 online shopping was available only in some areas within the area ringed by the M25 and will be in other areas 'soon'. There is a local delivery charge of £5. You can take a tour of the site, but a warning notice said: 'The shop is loading for you. This may take 3 to 5 minutes but you'll then be able to shop quickly from the full Sainsbury's to You range.' It seemed a long wait, sitting in front of a computer, but of course it could take you that long to walk from your car to inside the store. In the store area you can click to start with various pre-selected lists of products, to quick-start a new shopping trolley.

*Somerfield*
http://www.somerfield.co.uk/
Another well known UK high street name has entered the fray. You can shop in-store and they'll deliver your groceries to your home. The site enables you to find a local store that runs the scheme. Delivery is free when you spend over £25 in one transaction and live within the designated postcode area, otherwise charges may apply. Its special temperature-controlled vans help ensure freshness and that frozen goods stay frozen. The offer does not include fuel, cigarettes, tobacco, lottery tickets and scratchcards, infant formula, medicines and vitamins, postage and saving stamps, gift vouchers, rotisserie, phone cards or Vodafone top-up cards. We were impressed with a well-written cookery class and over 200 accompanying recipes to try. The site also gives details of more than 400 wines. You can browse through five sections here – world of wine, instant expert, best cellars, wine list and party time. If your speakers are switched on, you can even improve your accent with its talking pronunciation guide, ready to impress at parties.

*Tesco*
http://www.tesco.co.uk/
With its impressive web site, Tesco appears to have taken the lead in the battle for online customers in the UK. It says it is adding five stores per week to its delivery areas. Tesco has clearly identified a growing market in online convenience shopping, and are reacting to it rapidly and positively, as it has to great social changes in the past, such as the rise of the motor car. The site is backed up with a host of services such as Tesconet, SchoolNet, its computers for schools programme, customer services information, graduate recruitment, and finance packages. It also offers a useful net guide, and a general site search facility.

# Food and drink...........................................................................

Fig. 62. The grocery supermarket chain Tesco has developed a substantial web site. It clearly shows the importance it attaches to online retailing and customer services for the future.

*Waitrose*

http://www.waitrose.co.uk/

This is a pleasing-looking site which downloads quickly. Waitrose even offers its own free ISP connection software available, which you can download and use to access the internet. At present, Waitrose Direct on-line shopping offers a restricted range of items – wines, organics, flowers and gifts – delivered direct to your door. It also sells books, CDs and videos, and has a link to online travel bookings. It is making use of some top names in the food industry, such as top chef Raymond Blanc. Waitrose is associated with the John Lewis Partnership.

## Wines, beers and spirits

*AmiVin*

http://www.amivin.com

AmiVin is a top online wine merchant offering fine wines for gifts, collectors and everyday drinking at home. It is a wholly owned subsidiary of Fine and Rare Wines Ltd, the international London-based fine wine brokers. The chairman, Mark Bedini is quoted as saying: 'The internet brings so much flexibility and possibilities of working with partners in a way that just didn't exist before and this makes so much more achievable. You ain't see nothing yet!' The site is well designed and well worth exploring to track down and learn more about your favourite wines. The site offers an associates programme whereby if you link your site to theirs, and they obtain business as a result, you can earn a commission.

Fig. 63. Waitrose is another contender in the online grocery stakes. It is broadening the appeal of its web site with a restaurants guide, news updates, travel, health and beauty, education and other sections.

### Bibendum Wine

http://www.bibendum-wine.co.uk/

Bibendum is one of the UK's leading independent wine merchants. The business was started in 1984 by a small group of friends, using a shop in Primrose Hill village, north London. It is now one of the UK's top online wine merchants. It offers a free home delivery service covering not just London but the whole of England and Wales. The site has a phone number you can call if you want to talk to a real person. Check out the site for details of wine tastings.

### Bin Club

http://www.binclub.co.uk/

The Bin Club was started in 1977, by Jim Hood, as a way of helping people who live abroad to develop their own wine cellar in the UK. Today the club has membership in 70 countries and looks after some 30,000 cases of wine in its own cellars. For a monthly fee you can build up your account and the experts will help you choose some high quality wines. You can even arrange to have wine laid down for future generations. Once you have wines in your account, Bin Club can arrange to have then delivered to any mainland UK address while you are visiting Britain. The design of the site is delightful, with a background pattern suggesting a wine crate.

### Best Cellars

http://www.devon.directory.co.uk/bestcellars/

Best Cellars is a Devon-based company formed in 1989. It aims to introduce you to the finest wines from around the world. When we visited, it had wines from the Champagne region of France on offer, together with a large range of South African wines. Available in single or mixed cases, it also has wines from Argentina, Australia, Chile, England, France, Germany, Hungary, Italy, Portugal, Spain and New Zealand. It has online ordering facilities, which it says are secure.

# Food and drink...........................................................

*Bollinger – Champagne*
http://www.bollinger.co.uk
One of the top French champagnes, 'Bolly' became well-known to the wider public some years ago as the champagne of James Bond, and more recently of the girls in *Absolutely Fabulous*. It is one of the last champagne houses to mature in barrels. Check out its Special Cuvée Brut, Grande Année Brut, Bollinger Rosé and other tempting offerings. There are links to products, ethics, the family, vineyards, techniques, a newsletter, and the future, but to buy you'll have to visit a retailer.

*Bordeaux Wines*
http://www.bordeaux.com
This easy-to-use and expert site demystifies Bordeaux wines, with lots of fun information and wine tips along the way, such as wine fundamentals, buying for home, ordering in restaurants, reading a label, food and wine harmony, and tasting tips. The site includes explanations of the grape varieties, appellations, vintage charts, a wine glossary and details of the Bordeaux official classifications. You can find out how to plan a Bordeaux party and choose and order the appropriate wines. The site downloads quickly, and opens with some animated graphics that you can skip if you wish. The service runs tours of the Bordeaux region of France where you can taste the wine and learn about different grape varieties. If you enjoy fine wine and are keen to learn more about the wines and how they are made, this is well worth a look.

*Bulgarian Wines*
http://www.bulgarianwine.com
The site is a development of the Bulgarian Wine Guild, which aims to improve awareness of Bulgarian wines in the UK. There are links to market information, the web site, annual trade tastings, club tastings, a newsletter (*Nazdrave*), media relations and promotions, membership of the Guild, stockist information, plus background and travel information.

*CAMRA*
http://www.camra.org.uk/
This is the virtual home of the UK Campaign for Real Ale, complete with details of membership, beer festivals, brewery information, real ale guide, campaign information and more.

*Chateau Online*
http://www.chateauonline.co.uk/
This is an independent commercial site which offers a choice of nearly 1,400 wines, selected by Jean-Michel Deluc, a former Head Sommelier from the Paris Ritz. It aims to offer excellent service in the wine business. The pages can be viewed in English, French, and German. It has an enormous variety of wines and wine types on offer, including champagnes. You can search by price and keyword. Customers can benefit from regular special offers, which it claims are among the most competitive available. Chateau Online will deliver throughout the countries of the European Union. In the UK, it says delivery is from one to three weeks. A flat-

Fig. 64. Chateau Online is one of an increasing number of online wine merchants. You can find out a great deal about the different wines and wine-making methods from web sites like these.

rate delivery charge of £5.99 is made irrespective of the size of the order. The site includes a gift shop, and a newsletter which they can email to you.

*Corney & Barrow*
http://www.corbar1.demon.co.uk/
Corney & Barrow is an old-established London firm of independent wine merchants, It has come a long way since it first began to sell porter, old sack, and clarets in 1780. It has close ties with Bordeaux and Burgundy in France, and with Portugal, which means it can offer some of the finest wines around. The site includes quality information on each type of wine it offers. Petrus for example was covered in real depth. What the site lacks in sophistication is makes up for with authoritative advice and selections.

*Deutsche Weine im Internet*
http://www.weine.de
The name means German Wine on the Internet. You will need to be able to read German to view it properly.

*Enjoyment*
http://www.enjoyment.co.uk/
We came across this site as a result of following a link to Victoria Wine, the off-licence retailer with more than 1,500 shops across the UK. Using the web site you can order wine by the case, for free delivery. However, when we inspected the site, no wine was available because they were updating their lists.

# Food and drink...........................................................

## Eton Vintners
http://www.etonvintners.co.uk/
Eton Vintners sell quality wines, ports, armagnacs and cognacs. This is a delightful-looking site, run by a small company based in Windsor, established in 1985. It has some excellent wines and spirits selections, and also offers hampers, gift boxes and baskets to suit all tastes and budgets. The site includes a wine finder service, which they say can locate any wine right back to 1900.

## Gosset Champagnes
http://www.gosset.com
Since 1584, the family's savoir-faire has been passed down from generation to generation. Today, Gosset champagnes are renowned for their quality, delicacy and personality. Designed in black and gold, this expensive-looking web site tells you about the history of the company, and the products for which it is famous. It can be read in English, French and Spanish.

## Hatch Mansfield
http://www.hatchmansfield.com
With former links to Grants of St James, Hatch Mansfield is a UK distribution company formed by three commercial partners, Louis Jadot, Errazuriz (Chile) and Villa Maria. Among the great names which the company represents are the Esk Valley Estate (New Zealand), Caliterra (Chile), Sena (Chile), St Francis (USA) and Taittinger (France).

## Lindemanns
http://www.lindemans.com
The well-designed but slow-loading pages of the Lindemanns site tell you all about the originals and activities of this Australian winemaker. Cawarra Claret was the first wine to be exported by Dr Lindeman, a British navy surgeon, in 1858. The current range of Cawarra wines depict the homestead on the label. The company's products include Hunter River and Coonawarra, and it also produces a range of ports and desert wines.

## Martinez Bujanda
http://www.martinezbujanda.com
This Spanish winegrower was founded over a century ago in Riaja Alavesa by Joaquín Martínez Bujanda. The grapes come exclusively from the family's own vineyards, 400 hectares in the three sub-regions of Rioja Alta, Rioja Alavesa and Rioja Baja. The predominantly red grape varieties grown are Tempranillo, Mazuelo, Garnacha, and Cabernet Sauvignon. The whites include Viura and Malvasia. The site can be viewed in Spanish, English and German.

## Moët & Chandon – Champagne
http://www.champagne.com
This is the web site of France's best-known champagne maker, Moët & Chandon, popular in England and consumed in vast quantities at British weddings. One wonders how much it cost the company to acquire the

domain name champagne.com? Its products range from Brut Impérial and Brut Rosé, to White Star and Nectar Impérial. The firm was founded in 1743. Click La Boutique to order both wines and gifts online.

### Mumm's – Champagne
http://www.mumm.com
This is the web site of the famous French champagne-maker, based in Reims. 'If you are an adult of legal drinking age, we invite you to visit our sites.' Younger people probably would not have the patience to wait for the graphics-heavy site to download. The company is represented in the UK by Seagrams in Hammersmith, London. The wines on offer include Mumm Cordon Rouge 1995, Cuvée Limitée 1990, Cordon Rouge, and Mumm de Cramant.

### New Zealand Wines
http://www.nzwine.com
This is an official web site for the New Zealand wine and grape industry. They say that the growing recognition for its Chardonnay, Pinot Noir, Méthode Traditionelle sparkling wines, Riesling, Cabernet Sauvignon and Merlot blends is helping to further cement New Zealand's reputation as a producer of world-class wines. You can find out more about its wine styles, regions, wineries, wine news, and other information.

### Penfolds
http://www.penfolds.com
Penfolds is a very well known and successful Australian wine grower and shipper, whose white and red wines are widely available in British super-stores and off-licences. While you can't buy here, the site does offer some quite detailed description of dozens of its individual products – Bin 389 Cabernet Shiraz, Bin 407 Cabernet Sauvignon, Koonunga Hill Semillon Sauvignon Blanc, and dozens of others.

### Pubworld
http://www.pubworld.co.uk/
This is a great source of information about pubs, breweries, beers, sup-pliers and other aspects of the UK brewing industry. You can visit the Virtual Bar, where you can send a friend a virtual drink and a private message, collect a virtual drink and private message, and enjoy a drink on the house. The site includes some useful directories. There is one for brewers (from Abbey to Yukon), one for retailers, and a directory of the main owners of the pub groups.

### Rosemount Estates
http://www.rosemountestates.com.au
Everything you want to know about the Australian company Rosemount, its history, grape varieties, vineyards and wine-making. You can explore its varietals, sparkling wines, premium and flagship wines, and critical views and news.

# Food and drink...........................................................................

*Scotch Malt Whisky Society*
http://www.smws.com/
This is the virtual home of an association of lovers of single malt Scotch whisky. The site includes archives of articles from the Society's newsletters. plus a good selection of links to sites of related interest – organisations, distilleries, general and even literature.

*South African Wines*
http://www.intewine.co.uk/
Established on the net since 1995, InteWine is a family-owned company selling South African wines both on and off the internet. Its top 165 wines are listed by wine and by vineyard. There are two wine distributors, one in London and the other in Cape Town.

*Taittinger – Champagne*
http://www.taittinger.com
There is something here for the more experienced champagne drinker interested in exploring the history of this famous French family business which traces its origins back to 1734. You can take a cellar tour, view biographies, and of course find out about its individual champagnes. The site can be viewed in both French and English.

*Unwins Wine Merchants*
http://www.unwins.co.uk/
Unwins is a leading UK chain of high street off-licences, selling wines, spirits and other items. We found a good page of wines, all priced below £10. However, the site was being reconstructed and no information was available.

*Veuve Clicquot – Champagne*
http://www.veuveclicquot.co.uk
This is the home page of Veuve Clicquot ('the Widow Cliquot'), another top French producer of fine champagnes, founded before the French Revolution in 1772 The site can be read in French, English and Spanish. For ordering you will need to visit a high street or online retailer.

*Whisky Shop*
http://www.whiskyshop.com/
The Whisky Shop is a specialist whisky retailer offering malt, blended, rare, and liqueur whiskies. All orders on this efficient-looking site are encrypted before being sent to them by a secure server, or you can order by post or fax.

*Wine Cellar*
http://www.winecellar.co.uk/
There is an impressive first-time visitor page on this site. We loved the comic graphics. There was an animated drinker who, when clicked on, also served as a navigation tool. This is an impressive site design, combining entertainment and functionality. Its search facility for beers, wines and even cigars worked well. Details of their whiskies were well set out.

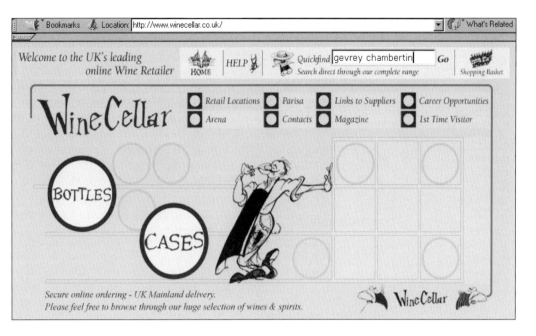

| | |
| --- | --- |
| Bookmarks | Location: http://www.winecellar.co.uk/ | What's Related |

Welcome to the UK's leading
online Wine Retailer · HOME · HELP · Quickfind gevrey chambertin · Go · Shopping Basket
Search direct through our complete range

WineCellar

○ Retail Locations   ○ Parisa   ○ Links to Suppliers   ○ Career Opportunities
○ Arena   ○ Contacts   ○ Magazine   ○ 1st Time Visitor

BOTTLES

CASES

Secure online ordering - UK Mainland delivery.
Please feel free to browse through our huge selection of wines & spirits.   WineCellar

We also liked their Review function, which enables you to track your order as you progress through the site.

Fig. 65. Wine Cellar is another UK-based wine retailer whose web site is well worth a visit.

*Wines on the Internet*
http://www.wines.com/
This American site contains some useful listings of wine events, lots of resources and information to help learn more about wines, a virtual tasting room and virtual wineries. Although the graphics take a little while to download, it's worth the wait. It has some great links to other virtual winery web sites around the world, for example to Marquis Alfieri. We found lots of books about wine for sale here, a US magazine called *Wine Trader*, and some articles by James Mead, called Mead on Wine. The site is worth a visit, not least for its many worldwide wine links.

## Food and wine magazines

*Diabetic Gourmet*
http://www.diabeticgourmet.com/
Diabetic Gourmet is a nicely-presented monthly online magazine dedicated to healthy eating, living, and gourmet topics for a diabetic audience.

*Epicurus Online*
http://www.epicurus.com/
This is an established food, beverage, and travel ezine for both consumers and professionals. The site includes a food glossary, bookstore, cookbook, discussion forums, a culinary quotes slideshow, culinary quotes, postcards, chat rooms, a post office, and events calendar.

# Food and drink......................................................................

Fig. 66. Epicurus is an established American online service for anyone seriously interested in food and cookery.

*Food and Drink Online*
http://www.foodanddrink.co.uk/
This a web site linked to the UK trade journals *The Grocer* and *Off Licence News*. It includes industry news and events, company and product databases, and is intended as a communications hub for the UK food and drink industry. Free registration is required.

*Vegetarian Times*
http://www.vegetariantimes.com
A useful source of recipes, resources and information, bulletin boards and links can be found here.

*Vinosearch*
http://www.vinosearch.com/magazines.htm
An excellent facility enables you to browse to more than 70 different wine magazines all over the internet. Highly recommended.

*Wine and Dine*
http://www.winedine.co.uk/
First published in 1995, *Wine and Dine* claims to have been the first British electronic magazine on wine, food and travel. Recent features have included makers of Chile's best red, summer wine tastings, phylloxera-resistant vines, the gin sling, cocktail of the month, and Bordeaux's finest.

*Wine Pages*
http://www.wine-pages.com
Written by a UK wine journalist and consultant, this useful site offers a mass of independent and non-commercial wine news, reviews, and suggestions – well worth a look.

# 9 Lifestyle

**In this chapter we will explore:**

- ▶ *clothes and fashion*
- ▶ *beauty products*
- ▶ *health and well-being*
- ▶ *flowers, gifts and accessories*
- ▶ *holidays and travel*
- ▶ *mobile phones*

. . . . . . . . . . . . . . . . . . . . . . . . . . . . . . . . . . . . . . . . . . . . . . . . . . . . . . . . . . . .

## Clothes and fashion

*Austin Reed*
http://www.austinreed.co.uk/
The site offers periodic seasonal reductions in men's tailoring. When reviewed there was no online ordering, and the web site was being used as an advertisement to encourage people to phone the company's customer service department or request a brochure. The company also offers a range of women's wear.

*Benetton*
http://www.benettononline.com
This is the web site of the Benetton retail chain, which offers knitwear and clothing for adults and children. The site was still being developed when reviewed.

Fig. 67. Visit the stylish web site of Christian Dior for a glimpse of some great fashion ideas.

*Burton*

http://www.burtonmenswear.co.uk

Burtons is a high street retailer selling clothes for men. The group actually owns a number of well-known brands such as Principles, Top Man and Top Shop, and Dorothy Perkins. Links will take you to each of its brand web sites. Each store site provides information about its own product lines, prize competitions, feedback, account card application requests and online shopping areas (still under development when reviewed).

*Diesel*

http://www.diesel.com

Diesel has won a following with fashion-conscious high street shoppers, and is embracing internet technology. On its cool-looking web site you can track your order, make enquiries, comments or suggestions, consult the FAQs, and join the Diesel Club. Diesel aims to dispatch all online orders within a week. Payment pages are held on Netbanx Online Bank secure servers. Diesel itself does not require. and is not provided with. any customer card details.

*Dior*

http://www.dior.com/

Christian Dior of Paris is a famous producer of fashion, cosmetics, fragrances and skin care products for both men and women. Its glossy and expensive-looking web site includes flash and audio (music) effects. The site offers customer registration: 'If you are not already a Mydior member, compose Your Look and enjoy a Diorissima world.'

*Dorothy Perkins*

http://www.dorothyperkins.co.uk

This is the cyber-home of the well-known high street women's fashion retailer. In common with other divisions of the Burtons group, the company has developed a good-looking and interactive web site some way ahead of many of its UK competitors. There are links to online shopping, looks, services, petites, and maternity, as well as to company information. You can sign up to receive the its email newsletter.

*Evans*

http://www.evans.ltd.uk

Evans is an established women's clothes retailer. On its forward-looking web site you will find prize quizzes, a sizing guide and news by email. You can sign up for an account card, order a catalogue, and of course browse through the various well-presented online fashion pages. The site includes a feature called Quickshop where you can order an item over the internet from the catalogue by typing its product code into a box. Orders can be taken for delivery worldwide. As a registered user you will save time online because your details will automatically appear in the ordering form each time you visit.

*Gap*

http://www.gap.com/

From jeans and T-shirts to khakis and jackets, Gap offers modern and seasonal styles in a clean organized, easy-to-shop environment. Its merchandise ranges from clothing and accessories to personal care products for adults, kids and babies. The chain extends across more than 1,800 stores in the US, Canada, France, Germany, Japan and the UK. The stylish-looking site provides access to Gap, GapKids, Baby Gap, and Gap Outlet stores. The site includes a store locator.

### Henry Poole of Savile Row
http://www.pooles-of-savile-row.co.uk
Henry Poole & Co is a long-established firm of gentlemen's custom tailors and bespoke outfitters who have been in business since 1806. Why not treat yourself to a handmade suit from this famous edge-of-Mayfair street in London?

### Lacoste
http://www.lacoste.com
The famous sportswear brand has built an impressive-looking web site of information for consumers. The company's founder, René Lacoste, was a French tennis champion who won the French Open three times and Wimbledon twice, and took the Davis Cup away from the Americans in 1927. He was nicknamed 'the Alligator' by the American press, hence the distinctive little green motif you see on Lacoste products.

### Lands' End
http://www.landsend.com
Lands' End is a well-known American company that sells a large range of women's, men's and children's fashion internationally. This impressive-looking site knocks spots off those of most of its competitors. Its depth and quality, and highly professional design, shows just how far UK and European companies will have to go to catch up in serving the online consumer market.

### Moss Bros
http://www.mossbros.com
Moss Bros is a famous menswear retail and hire group aimed at targeted at the more traditional segments of the UK market. Its brand names include Moss Bros, The Savoy Taylors Guild, Beale & Inman, Cecil Gee, Blazer and The Suit Company. Its brands reflect classic, fashion and mainstream aspects of the menswear market.

### Next
http://www.next.co.uk
Next is a prominent UK high street fashion retailer for both sexes and all ages. It also sells some household goods. You can now shop online, browsing through and choosing from over 1,300 styles. You can order with Quick Shop by entering item numbers from any of its current catalogues. You will need to register for a Next Directory Flexible Account. This can be set up online immediately and gives you instant credit so you can start shopping straight away. Keen for your business, the site offers next day delivery and a free open returns policy.

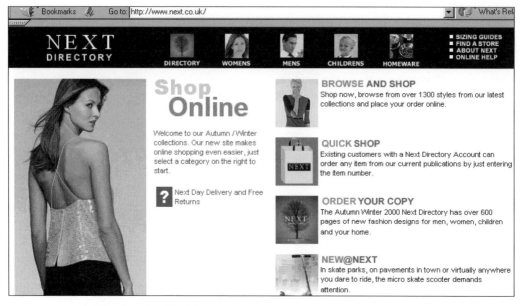

Fig. 68. The web site of Next, the UK high street fashion retailer. Here you can easily browse through 1,300 different styles from the comfort of your own home.

*Paul Smith*

http://www.paulsmith.co.uk/

This is the web site of the menswear label owned by the recently knighted designer Sir Paul Smith. A hands-on manager, he has eight shops in London, one in Manchester, one in New York, one in Paris, five in Hong Kong, two in Singapore, four in Taiwan, one in Manila, the original shop in Nottingham, and a staggering 200 shops in Japan. Viewing this stylish site (which you can also do in Japanese) requires the Shockwave Flash plugin.

*Principles*

http://www.principles.co.uk

Principles is a ladies and gents fashion store, and an associated brand of Burtons. 'If you want to go shopping you can browse the store by department and by item. If you're in a hurry there's also a Fast Index which will show you a text listing of all the styles available today. If you have a copy of our latest catalogue you can shop by entering the product code here, or use the Fastrack order form.'

*Rive Gauche*

http://www.rivegauche.co.uk/

Rive Gauche takes its name from the trendy Left Bank area of the River Seine in Paris. This stylish-looking site represents an array of top names in the fashion world such as Louis Feraud, Yves St Laurent, and Mondi and displays about twenty exciting collections in elegant surroundings. You cannot, however, order online; the site is in effect a glossy brochure with very little interactivity or ancillary features.

*Savile Row: The Webzine for Gentlemen*
http://www.savilerow.com
This is a webzine for men's fashion, wardrobe, grooming, etiquette, including articles and tips on gifts for men. It contains information about the finest in gentleman's tailoring, jewellery, cologne, leather goods, toiletries, furniture and toys.

*Shoeworld*
http://www.shoeworld.com/
This is a substantial UK consumer and retail information web site, giving lots of information about the major brands and manufacturers. It says it is the UK's largest footwear website. There are loads of links, guides to footwear fashion, online shopping facilities, and you can even use the site to design your own footwear.

Fig. 69. Shoeworld is one of the most comprehensive web sites around for footwear. It covers products, services, suppliers, news, industry information and lots more.

*Tee Finder*
http://www.teefinder.com/
Have you got a favourite band, or TV show? Here is something out of the ordinary, an internet search engine specially created to help you find and obtain specific T-shirts.

*Top Man*
http://www.topman.co.uk
Topman is an associated brand of Burtons. You can browse its youth-oriented online store and check out the latest styles. This animated, colourful and streetwise web site even includes a dating board. They say: 'We've cut away all that five-day delivery nonsense and provided you order before 3pm Monday to Friday we'll send by next day courier service.'

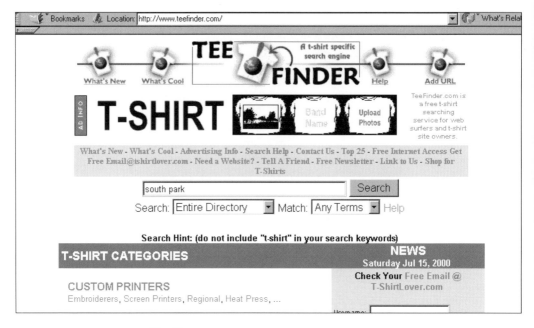

Fig. 70. Tee-Finder must be the ultimate web site for T-shirt junkies.

## Top Shop

http://www.tops.co.uk

You can browse the online store using this browse online store link or look at its inspiration section for a one-page reference for each current trend. There is helpful guidance on how to add items to your shopping basket, and on how the whole online shop works. Top Shop is part of the Arcadia Group – the second largest retailer in the UK. The site offers fully secure online transactions and accepts Visa, MasterCard, Switch, and other account cards. There is a simple refund and exchange policy, and can even make returns to your local store.

*See also* – shops and stores in chapter 5.

## Beauty products

*Avon*

http://www.avon.com

This is a good-looking site which leads you to an online shop, tips and ideas, and company background. A Virtual Beauty Advisor offers advice on how choose the best colours and products. You complete and submit an online questionnaire, and an answer comes back immediately with the colours that are right for your eyes, cheeks and lips. There is information about various weekly specials. Topics include aromatherapy, makeup, subscription offers, perfume, and tips and ideas for enhanced health and beauty. The site includes a search engine.

*Balmain*

https://www.luxelle.com/splash.html

Balmain of Paris is a prestigious supplier of French cosmetics and skin care products. Its clients include many of the most famous, elegant and prominent women in the world including first ladies, celebrities and royalty. Here you can find out about Pierre Balmain himself, who designed for stage and screen, creating personal wardrobes for many international movie stars. He also became the personal couturier to queens and princesses from royal families around the world.

### Chanel
http://www.chanel.com/
This is the place to explore Chanel, from its French founder Coco Chanel to Lagerfeld, the legend and story. The site includes three links to fashion topics – an haute couture show, a ready-to-wear show, and links to Chanel Vision – and to a skincare page called Chanel Précision. However, the site was in the course of development when reviewed.

### Clinique
http://www.clinique.com/
This is a substantial web site with a host of features ranging from a gift centre, foundation finder, a bridal guide, FAQs, an acne problem solver, beauty workshops and more.

### Cosmetics Boutique
http://www.cosmeticsboutique.com/
Cosmetics Boutique is a bright-looking online cosmetics store. It also provides links to the best places on the net for purchasing and reading about cosmetics. The company is located in San Diego, California.

### Cover Girl
http://www.covergirl.com/
The Cover Girl web site offers instant personal recommendations on your right make-up and shades, together with beauty advice, and details of what's new in cosmetics and fashion. Cover Girl is a division of Procter & Gamble.

### I-Beauty Cosmetics Counter
http://www10.ibeauty.com/index.jsp
At this professional-looking US web site you can shop online for leading brand name cosmetics such as Estée Lauder, Clinique, Lancôme, or Elizabeth Arden. All credit card transactions on its web site are protected by secure server software. The site benefits from some very clearly set out FAQs explaining the ordering and delivery procedure for you.

### Independent Cosmetic Manufacturers and Distributors
http://www.icmad.org/
ICMAD is an international trade association of more than 600 small, entrepreneurial companies, representing virtually all segments of the cosmetic and beauty industry. If you are looking for a specialist product, you might find it somewhere here.

HOME
FASHION
. Haute Couture Show
. Ready-to-Wear Show
. CHANEL Vision

SKINCARE
. CHANEL PRÉCISION

*Lancôme*
http://www.lancome.com/
You can't buy its products online, but there is a store locator showing your nearest supplier. On the web site you can find out about the right skincare products for you and how to apply them, and consult their makeup tips and tricks of the trade so that you're always looking your best.

*L'Oréal*
http://www.lorealparisusa.com/
Whether you're inside or outdoors this season, you can apply skin-friendly advice from the skincare and suncare experts of this top supplier. For updates on news and features, you can subscribe to the L'Oréal email newsletter.

*Revlon*
http://www.Revlon.com
Revlon online offers an extensive array of cosmetics and skin care, fragrance, personal care products, and hair and nail care products. They are mainly intended for use in and resale by professional salons. Its broad range of cosmetics and skin care products tend to be priced in the upper range. It makes lip makeup, nail colour and nail care products, eye and face makeup and skin care products including lotions, cleansers, creams, toners and moisturisers.

## Health and well-being

*The Body Shop*
http://www.the-body-shop.com
The Body Shop's home page offers a virtual makeover, a bodyzine, company information, advice on well-being, and of course its products. A virtual makeover section advises you how to create the latest looks using the shop's products. This may take a minute or two to download. Each look has a variety of models so that all skin types are represented. The bodyzine contains articles about the company's products and services. A products page offers information about products, grouped by bath/shower, face care, skin care etc. Products are not yet offered online.

*Condom.co.uk*
http://www.condom.co.uk
Never feel embarrassed at buying 'protection' in a pharmacy again. This is one of several such UK sites offering a large range of products, together with secure online ordering.

*Health and Fitness Arcade*
http://www.crystalspirit.com/health/
The opening page on their site says: 'Join our mailing list for our new, free monthly newsletter with latest developments and an easy step by step guide if you really want to change to a sensible, happy and healthy lifestyle!' It has a huge graphic on the first page and took a while to download, so be patient.

*Health Shop*

http://www.thehealthshop.co.uk

This is a bright and bold site that claims to offer you the best value range of vitamins, minerals and food supplements. Its web shop has 'secure server' ordering for peace of mind. It also offers answers to frequently asked questions and information about themselves as a shop online. This site is ideal for those with a hectic lifestyle, but who still care about their physical condition.

*Hello Baby*

http://www.hellobaby.com/

Do you want to get pregnant using the internet? Well, you could, using the online sperm bank of a company like Pacific Reproductive Services. Female visitors to the site are invited to browse the donor profiles before making their selection. Pacific say: 'We remain committed to providing our children, upon adulthood, with the option of receiving information about their biological heritage.' Could millions of would-be mothers be routinely shopping for sperm in the future, with the prices based on the DNA and genetic profiles?

Fig. 71. Will shopping for babies on the internet one day become routine? Run by Pacific Reproductive services, Hello Baby offers an online sperm bank with donor details.

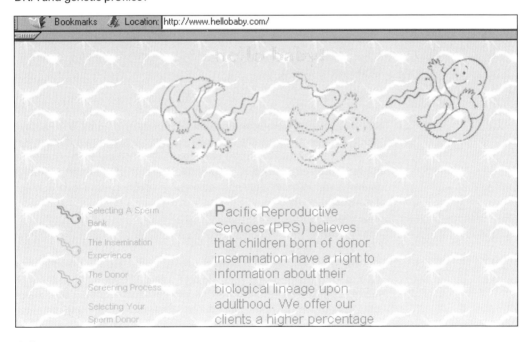

*Relate*

http://www.relate.org.uk/

Relate is Britain's leading 'couple-counselling' agency. Its web site offers high-quality counselling, relationship education and training to support couple and family relationships throughout life. You can purchase books on any aspect of personal relationships, explore news updates, and check out a list of all local centres so you know where to get in touch. The site also provides links to other useful sources for successful relationship management.

*Slimming World*
http://www.slimming-world.co.uk/
Slimming World is the largest independent slimming organisation in the UK and they believe in 'turning dreams into reality.' This fun and exciting site provides information about eating plans, how to join one of the 5,500 classes nationwide, postal membership, recent publications, and even career opportunities You can also find out about hair and beauty here.

*Weight Watchers UK*
http://uk.weightwatchers.com/
For over 30 years, Weight Watchers have been helping people in Britain to lose weight and stay slim. In the 6,000 meetings that take place every week, thousands of dieters find the support, motivation and information they need to achieve their goal weight. The site offers information about the meetings and what happens when you join, and information on their 'best diet ever'. There is news and special offers, and an online forum where you can post messages to other dieters, exchange recipes, make friends, and find inspiration and mutual support.

▶ *See also – Medicine & Health on the Internet* by Sarah Wilkinson in this series.

## Children's wear

*Mothercare*
http://www.mothercare.co.uk/
Mothercare sells clothes and supplies for pregnant mums, babies, and young children. The web site was still under development when reviewed in summer 2000, but the home page promises to provide a vast network of information covering all aspects of family life including health and child development. With its trusted brand name, it could attract a lot of interest if it succeeds in this.

*Tots to Teens*
http://www.tots2teens.co.uk/
The company is known for children's wear, supplying top brand names such as Ben Sherman, Kickers, Ralph Lauren, Ellesse and Adidas. The web site offers hundreds of items, secure transactions, and global delivery. The company is a division of Great Universal Stores.

## Flowers, gifts, and accessories

*GemNet*
http://www.gemnet.co.uk/
Established in 1992, and based in the Cotswolds, GemNet claims to be the largest English-speaking jewellery resource on the internet. It has around 30,000 products from a range of high street jewellery retailers, and offers secure online ordering. Drop-down menus enable you to shop by price, or by occasion (anniversary, barmitzvah, wedding and other events).

*Interfashion.net*
http://www.interfashion.net
This is an information source for the fashion industry, including houses and designers, manufacturers, events, photographers and more.

*Jewellers Net*
http://www.jewellers.net/
This British site offers a database of retailers searchable by geographic location, as well as general information about gold, amber, platinum, and diamonds. You can browse and purchase from over 1,800 ideas from gold and silver jewellery to luxury gift ideas and high quality watch brands such as Longines, Rotary and Citizen.

*Leather Net*
http://www.leathernet.com/
The Leather Net is dedicated to the leather industry worldwide. You can find out about footwear, furniture and all kinds of other leather-based products.

*Menswear UK*
http://www.menswear.co.uk/

*Flowers Direct*
http://www.flowersdirectuk.co.uk
You click on a bouquet icon to find more information about Flowers Direct. You can exoplore a catalogue which enables you to click the kind of flowers you are looking for: roses, arrangements, bouquets, vase flowers, and others. Or maybe there's a special occasion for which you need flowers: birthday, anniversary, thinking of you and special occasions. You can use its free email reminder for dates such as birthdays and anniversaries. There are photographs of the top sellers with short descriptions and prices, help with writing cards and general information on flowers.

*Get Well*
http://www.getwell.com/
GetWell is an American site which offers gift ideas for people who are sick or recovering in the hospital. If you are stuck for original ideas, some handy dropdown menus enable you to view suggested gifts relevant to the medical condition. You can also specify your relationship to the sufferer, and the sufferer's age.

*Global Gift Guide*
http://www.theggg.com/
The GGG offers guides to online stores all over the world, arranged by continent and country. It plans to include a Gift Alarm service to remind you of important dates for your diary.

*Interflora*
http://www.interflora.co.uk
Since early last century, Interflora has delivered a service like none other.

Bookmarks    Location: http://www.getwell.com/     What's Rel

home | health conditions | browse our gifts | send a care card | our partners | contact us | search

*from* **TYLENOL**

*GetWell.com*
Get informed... Send the perfect gift.

*It's Easy to Show You Care!*

• *Get Informed*
• *Send a Get Well Gift*
• *Send a Free Care Card*

Know somebody who's not feeling well or facing a serious illness? We make it easy to send a get well gift to brighten a loved one's day. Because the makers of TYLENOL® know that your thoughtfulness and personal attention can be powerful medicine.

GetWell Profiler

Get gift recommendations and customized information for your loved one.

Choose a condition...
Choose a relationship...
How old is the person?

Find

Caregiving Corner

Fig. 72. When choosing a card or gift it's the thought that counts, but using the menu options on the GetWell site they do the thinking to you save you time.

Starting with a fresh and original idea, it has become the world's largest and most popular flower delivery network. It is a non-profit making trade association owned by its member florists, and enabling 58,000 florists worldwide to deliver flowers to 146 countries. Local prices include VAT and a small service charge, which is slightly higher for deliveries made abroad. Major credit and debit cards are accepted.

*Watches of Switzerland*
http://www.w-o-s.com/
The site aims to build the most comprehensive directory of the watch industry on the internet. You will find recently published articles on watches and manufacturing of watches, a guide to high-tech watch sites, such as rotating watches, java watches, virtual watches, sound, movies, and a resources index. Any questions you may have on watches will probably find an answer here.

*Watchnet*
http://watchnet.com/
This Los Angeles site describes itself as the premier watch trading website. You can buy, sell and trade watches, clocks and timepieces, bands, tools, accessories, repairs, books and parts, and take part in online discussions.

*Who?*
http://www.whoapparel.co.uk/
Who? is a UK-based resource centre for the global fashion industry (mainly UK, Europe and the USA). Whether you want to track down a particular manufacturer, wholesaler or retailer, or supplier of a particular product or service, this is quite a good place to start looking. The informa-

tion is laid out in a functional way, and there are hyperlinks to many of the listed retailers.

### Worth Global Style Network

http://www.wgsn.com/

Here you will find interactive information for the fashion industry, including details of catwalk shows, graphics, resources and trends. Based at WGSN headquarters in London, and at its New York, Los Angeles, Paris and Tokyo offices, more than 100 creative and editorial staff work in co-operation with a growing WGSN network of photographers and research contributors around the world.

## Holidays and travel

### A to B Travel

http://www.a2btravel.com

This is probably the best travel site squarely primarily at British internet users. It is packed with information and useful hyperlinks to help you plan and enjoy your holiday. The site enables you to make travel bookings on-line, take advantage of last minute special offers, and arm yourself with up-to-date travel tips and news.

### British Tourist Authority

http://www.visitbritain.com/

They say: 'You may be planning a visit to Wimbledon, but what about the World Worm Charming, Toe Wrestling, Pea Shooting or Snail Racing Championships? Search our events database for information about these (and more mainstream!) events this summer.' This breezy site is packed with things to do and explore, and holiday suggestions for the jaded.

### The Daily Mail

http://www.thisistravel.com

This is a well-produced online consumer travel information service developed by *The Daily Mail*. Associated web pages include This is London, and This is Money.

### Fodors

http://www.fodors.com/

Fodors are publishers of a substantial series of travel guidebooks covering worldwide destinations. They are now making full use of internet technology. For example you can use the recently revamped web site to create your own online concise guide or guides to more than 160 destinations, view detailed maps, and swap stories with other travellers in its virtual travel lounge.

### Hotelworld

http://www.hotelworld.com

HotelWorld enables you to find, view and book hotels across the world. It contains information on nearly 9,000 hotels in 204 countries, all of which can be booked online. Information ranges from simple to comprehensive and may include a page listing room facilities and rates, and often a brochure with pictures.

*Lonely Planet*
http://www.lonelyplanet.com.au
Lonely Planet has built a solid reputation among independent travellers as a guidebook publisher. Its innovative and interactive web site lives up to its streetwise reputation.

*Map.com*
http://www.map.com/maps.html
With its animated graphics, the home page takes a little while to load, but when it does you will find it a valuable guide to thousands of online geographical and street maps of all kinds, covering all parts of the world.

*Microsoft Expedia*
http://expedia.msn.co.uk
This is one of the leading travel portal sites, and well worth exploring. It offers accommodation rental, adventure holidays, airport parking, foreign exchange, golfing holidays, Heathrow Express, last minute offers, low cost international calls, tax and duty free information, UK accommodation and a vast amount more.

*My Travel Guide*
http://www.mytravelguide.com
This is a substantial US information and portal site for world travel. The site includes a tour search web directory, a currency converter, language guide, driving directions, an interactive atlas, flight tracker, miles manager, travel planner, world clock and calendar, tours, a to-do list, free stuff, and series of public message and chat facilities.

*Netscape Travel*
http://www.netscape.com/travel/index.html
Netscape has developed its own substantial travel portal. There are handy links to air travel, car travel, lodging, vacations and cruises, bargains, business travel, local guides, destinations and many other essential topics.

*Overseas Airline Guides*
http://www.oag.com/tt/catalog/index.html
Best known for its immensely detailed flight guides, OAG Worldwide offers authoritative travel information for use in the office and on the road. Customers can access this information through media ranging from portable pocket guides and desktop references in print and electronic format, to a customised travel information system for use on a company's intranet or local area network.

*The Planet*
http://www.the-planet.co.uk
*The Planet* is an online UK database containing thousands of travel and

holiday reports from destinations around the world. The articles are gathered from the travel pages of *The Telegraph* newspaper.

*Rough Guides*
http://travel.roughguides.com/
Rough Guides are known for their comprehensive and contemporary coverage in paperback form of destinations far and wide from Amsterdam to Zimbabwe and 130 more in between. The web site mainly functions as an online brochure for their publications.

*Take Off*
http://www.takeoff.beeb.com/
This is a web site of the BBC. You can use it for finding late availability deals and special offers, finding a flight, booking online, looking for inspiration to find a holiday, win holidays worldwide, and join in news, views and exclusives (http://www.holiday.beeb.com/).

*The Travel Channel*
http://www.travelchannel.com/
The Discovery Travel Channel is another enormous travel portal site, which must surely contain the answer to just about every travel requirement and question.

*Travel File*
http://www.travelfile.com/
Travel File is a substantial online travel shopping resource that lets you plan at your leisure then book, pack and go! It is undoubtedly one of the top online travel information networks, available to some 450,000 travel agency terminals worldwide

*Travel Notes*
http://www.travelnotes.org
The site guides visitors to essential travel information, with the aid of detailed country backgrounds, reviewed web sites, and regular travel articles. The high editorial content of the site should make it of interest to the independent and long-haul traveller.

*Travelocity*
http://www.travelocity.com
Travelocity is one of the top travel sites providing secure online reservation capabilities for air, car, hotel and vacation reservations, plus access to a vast database of destination and other travel information. It offers reservations for 95 percent of all available airline seats, more than 47,000 hotels and more than 50 car rental companies. While booking your flight online you can even select specific seats for your flights with the aid of seat maps. The site also has street location maps and photos of selected hotels.

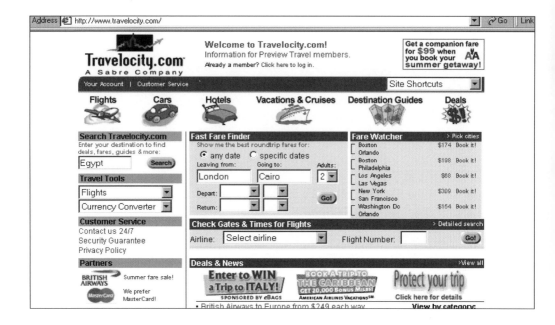

Fig. 73. Travelocity is one of the undoubted market leaders for online travel information.

*Virtual Tourist*

http://www.vtourist.com

This is another fantastic travel portal site, and well worth a look before you book.

▶ *See also – Travel & Holidays on the Internet*, Graham Jones (Internet Handbooks).

Fig. 74. At the Virtual Tourist web site you can browse through more than 30,000 possible travel destinations, interact with 70,000 other registered members, post notices, and receive travel alerts.

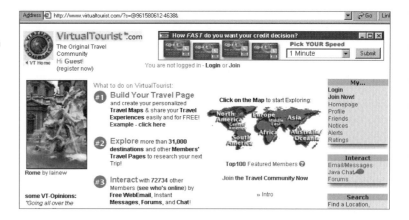

## Mobile phones

*One2one*
http://www.one2one.co.uk
One2one's bright, slick site is arranged to help you work out your best time plan, view its products, accessories, services and network coverage, and buy direct online. You can check out its price plans, optional services, and pay as you go. Should you decide you want to buy a phone, there is information on buying direct and finding a dealer. Be warned – some visitors may find that the site crashes when they visit new pages.

*Orange*
http://www.orange.co.uk
This site tells you all about Wirefree, Wildfire, Orange talk business, getting football results directly to your phone and many other Orange services. Information is further divided into how to buy, costs and kit, ownership and news. Buy online and Orange will deliver your phone for free, and throw in a car charger and free leather case. If you order specified models they will add a personal hands-free kit. You can buy Orange Just Talk online, with a choice of five phones. A map of the UK illustrates the network coverage.

*Vodafone*
http://www.vodafone.co.uk
Vodafone divides its site into three main profile areas: personal use, small business and large business. Each offers information on products, services, tariffs, coverage and purchases. You can win cinema tickets, return tickets to New York on Concorde, or a million air miles. Although the site initially downloads quickly, it takes a while to click from page to page. Once you have accessed a page the menus change. You can then find information on other topics such as rewards programmes, pocket radios, customer services, careers and business.

▶ *See also – Where to Find It on the Internet*, Kye Valongo (Internet Handbooks, 2nd edition).

# 10 Motors, caravans and boats

## In this chapter we will explore:

▶ *car magazines and advertising*

▶ *motoring information sites*

▶ *car manufacturers*

▶ *retail stores*

▶ *caravans and caravanning*

▶ *boats and boating*

. . . . . . . . . . . . . . . . . . . . . . . . . . . . . . . . . . . . . . . . . . . . .

## Car magazines and advertising

*Autoseek*
http://www.autoseek.co.uk/
The site says it has thousands of used cars for sale from all parts of the UK. If you wish to view them click Car Search. If you are a seller you can Sell For Free, or place a SuperAd. The latter includes the option of adding a photograph of your car, and getting it listed on Yahoo!Cars for maximum exposure. A useful feature of the site is its collection of links to hundreds of other useful motoring sites. These are conveniently arranged under parts and services, insurance, classic cars, car clubs and associations, motor sport, importing cars, car auctions and local services

Fig. 75. CarAds has around 16,000 passenger and commercial vehicles for sale in this well-organised database. You can limit your search to particular geographic areas.

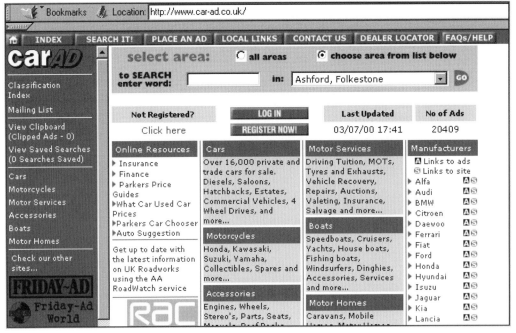

*Autotrader*

http://www.autotrader.co.uk/

Based on the illustrated magazine, Autotrader could fairly claim to be the top motoring web site in the UK with over 140,000 vehicles for sale, many of which are illustrated with colour photos. You can hunt for your next vehicle by exact make and model, or according to colour, price, mileage, age and how far you are prepared to travel to view. Once you have found the vehicle you want, Autotrader will step you through the buying process. It also has special offers, news, products, services and motoring advice. This is an impressively comprehensive site for someone looking for anything automotive. You can find information on auctions, dealers, hire and leasing and news and reviews. The site also has links to Norway, Belgium, South Africa and Italy.

*Car-Ad*

http://www.car-ad.co.uk/

The site is for reading and placing online car advertisements. It lists around 16,000 private and trade cars for sale – diesels, saloons, hatchbacks, estates, commercial vehicles, 4-wheel drives, and more. The site includes an RAC route-finder service; just type in your departure and destination locations, and the RAC will instantly calculate the fastest route, taking into account the latest Roadwatch traffic information. Other features of this substantial site include crash test results, information about international licences, car running costs, and personalised number plates.

*CarBuyer*

http://www.the-carbuyer.com/

The site offers free ads for the sale of cars and spare parts. You can add a colour photograph for a small fee. Its CarBuyer Directory contains some useful links to hundreds of UK car-related web sites

*Car Mailer*

http://www.carmailer.co.uk/

They say: 'Tell us about the kind of car that you are looking for and we will automatically email you details of exactly the type of car you are looking for when it becomes available. Every week we send out thousands of individually tailored emails to people all over the UK who are looking to buy their next car. Let us take the hassle of buying and selling. Register with us and we will keep you informed.' For a few pounds you can also advertise your own car for sale, – 'hold till sold' – and this will be included in the individually tailored emails they send out.

*CarSeller UK*

http://www.carseller.co.uk

CarSeller offers searchable databases of used car adverts and dealers, parts bulletin board, club links, and more. This is a free advert site and so is worthy of your consideration. It has a good list of available cars and a useful page of club links. Viewing the online clubs is a good way of both finding out what real owners think of their cars and perhaps to get access to parts.

# Motors, caravans and boats................................................

*Car Source*
http://www.carsource.co.uk/
Buying a new car, or even an ex-demonstrator or nearly new car? Before you do, it might be a good idea to check out this new car service, with its detailed specifications, photos and prices. The site also lists over 30,000 used cars online, so you could well find what you want here. It can also help you find cars that aren't listed. Car Source says it will contact up to seven dealers in an effort to find what you want. It may also be able to help you with finance. The service is free to private buyers. Click the link to Library, and you will also find used car prices, a used car model guide, car reviews, a car photo library, press releases, and other sites of interest.

*Dealer Deals*
http://www.dealerdeals.co.uk
This is a free email newsletter about the contract hire market in the UK. The company says it can find and deliver prestige vehicles, including to subscribers who are returning from overseas to the UK. Normally, the process for acquiring a prestige car involves waiting for the right advert to appear, with the right car at the right time. It will use a specialist on your behalf. You advise the specialist of your requirements, and the specialist will network to find the right vehicle for you. We checked the prices for prestige cars and they looked not unreasonable. If you are in the market for contract hire, this is worth a look.

*Easy Vehicle*
http://www.easyvehicle.com/
The site offers listings of cars, bikes, and vans. You can search for any vehicle based on your needs and specifications, whether it is price, special features or mileage, and narrow your search to the part of the country you live in. They say: 'We charge a one off registration fee of only £39.99 for you to use our service which puts your vehicle on our database and on the Internet, until your vehicle is sold. There are no further commissions or charges whatsoever.' You can also have your own web page on their web

Fig. 76. Exchange & Mart has one of the biggest online databases of motor vehicles for sale in the UK. The site includes a used car price guide, online insurance quotes from Screentrade, and advice for buyers.

146

site, with 250 characters of text and a free colour photo. There is a free-phone number to call.

## Exchange and Mart

http://www.ExchangeAndMart.co.uk/

*Exchange and Mart* is the UK's best-known weekly classified advertising magazine. This substantial web site offers a searchable database of motoring advertisements taken from the printed publication. There are usually around 50,000 used cars and 20,000 personalised number plates to choose from. They say: 'You must be a registered user to place an advert. Advertising via the internet is only available to private sellers All transactions are carried out over a secure Netbanx server. Once the transaction has been successfully completed, you will receive a confirmation email. Adverts do not appear instantly on the site. All adverts will appear online within 48 hours of submission. This excludes hold-till-sold ads, which take three to four working days to appear on the database.' The site includes a handy used car price guide.

## Fish4cars

http://www.fish4cars.co.uk/

Fish4 is a new grouping of four internet consumer web sites, three service sites and an online directory. Backed by the UK's regional press, the sites were launched in late 1999 and mark a major investment in interactive media. They include Fish4cars, Fish4jobs and Fish4homes. Fish4cars says it carries the largest database of used cars in the country – averaging between 180,000 and 200,000 vehicles at any one time. The site includes many useful features such as new and used car road tests, finance and insurance information.

Fig. 77. With support from local newspapers around the UK, Fish4cars has developed a big database of vehicles for sale around 180,000 in all. The web site has many motor-related features of interest.

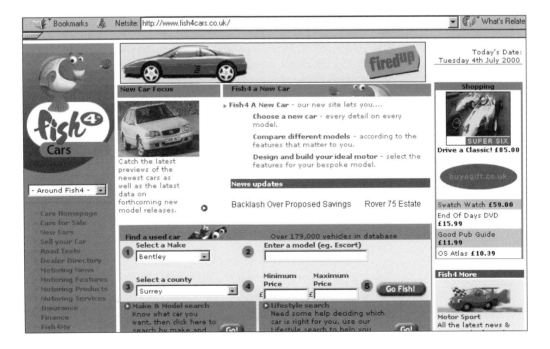

Simply select the make, model, derivative and year, type in the current mileage and the software does the rest! At the press of a button, you have single, well defined, trade and retail values - even the mileage adjustment is instant.

Plus, monthly update disks ensure you are always working with the very latest information. Having recently undergone considerable re-development, this PC-version of the UK's best-selling Valuation Guide now contains even more useful features to help you work efficiently.

- **New Car Prices**  Showing the list price, VAT and total price.
- **Used Vehicle Values**  Accurate values with automatic mileage adjustment.
- **Bespoke Reporting**  Allowing you to print exactly the information you need.
- **Trade Directory**  Alphabetical list of vehicle traders, listed by manufacturer.
- **Editorial**  Topical supply and demand issues, plus recent market trends.
- **News Flash**  Showing changes in the current month's cost new section.
- **Trend Analysis Graphing**  Showing how a vehicle's value changes over time.
- **Group Valuations**  Automatically analysing the vehicles of most interest to you.
- **Historical Data**  Easily retrievable for quick reference.

Fig. 78. Don't let the dealers run circles round you. Visit Glass's Guide online, and find out for yourself what your car is worth, and what you should be paying for a replacement vehicle.

*Glass's Guide*
http://www.glass.co.uk
This is the online version of the well-known trade publication that monitors price trends in the car market and can quote car values. They are very experienced in this, having done it since 1933, so whether you are trying to either buy or sell a vehicle, a visit to this site could pay dividends. There is now a PC version of the Guide supplied on monthly disks. The site includes a daily online newspaper called MotorTrader.Com.

*MotorTrak*
http://www.motortrak.com
Founded in 1995, MotorTrak brings together the resources of some of the leading UK motor manufacturers and dealers. Using this simple yet powerful database allows you to search for the car of your choice from franchised dealers only.

*NetCar*
http://www.netcar.co.uk
Here you can search for a vehicle, place your own ad, explore legal stuff, trade information, motor sport and other interesting links, sign a guest book, and browse through vehicles and parts for sale and wanted, and bargain vehicles. The site includes a forum, a help area, and an email facility. You can also search for your ultimate cherished number plate.

*Office of Fair Trading: Used Cars*
http://www.oft.gov.uk/html/cars/home.htm
This is a UK government site that aims to help people who are buying or selling cars for the first time. However, when reviewed some of the pages were unavailable. There is some forthright advice about (not) buying a stolen car. If you do buy a stolen car in good faith, you will lose the car

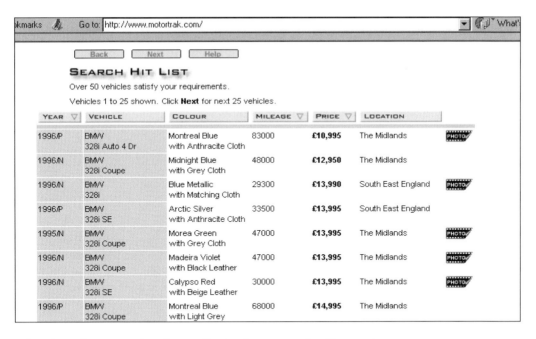

| | | | | | |
|---|---|---|---|---|---|
| | Back | Next | Help | | |

**SEARCH HIT LIST**

Over 50 vehicles satisfy your requirements.

Vehicles 1 to 25 shown. Click **Next** for next 25 vehicles.

| YEAR | VEHICLE | COLOUR | MILEAGE | PRICE | LOCATION | |
|---|---|---|---|---|---|---|
| 1996/P | BMW 328i Auto 4 Dr | Montreal Blue with Anthracite Cloth | 83000 | **£10,995** | The Midlands | PHOTO |
| 1996/N | BMW 328i Coupe | Midnight Blue with Grey Cloth | 48000 | **£12,950** | The Midlands | |
| 1996/N | BMW 328i | Blue Metallic with Matching Cloth | 29300 | **£13,990** | South East England | PHOTO |
| 1996/P | BMW 328i SE | Arctic Silver with Anthracite Cloth | 33500 | **£13,995** | South East England | |
| 1995/N | BMW 328i Coupe | Morea Green with Grey Cloth | 47000 | **£13,995** | The Midlands | PHOTO |
| 1996/N | BMW 328i Coupe | Madeira Violet with Black Leather | 47000 | **£13,995** | The Midlands | PHOTO |
| 1996/N | BMW 328i SE | Calypso Red with Beige Leather | 30000 | **£13,995** | The Midlands | PHOTO |
| 1996/P | BMW 328i Coupe | Montreal Blue with Light Grey | 68000 | **£14,995** | The Midlands | |

when the police recover it and you will not get compensation. You can try and recover some of your losses by suing the person who sold you the car, if you can find them.

*Online Cars UK*
http://www.online-cars.com/
Set up in 1998, this Yorkshire-based site offers a dealership finder, a used car database, free private advertising, some performance car information, find a number plate, details of forthcoming motoring events, and assorted car clubs news.

*Porsche Classifieds*
http://www.porsche-classified.co.uk
The site includes cars for sale, a price guide, bookshop, a message board, advice on insurance, accessories, dealers, events, repairs, club information, and links to other Porsche sites.

*Virgin Cars*
http://www.virgincars.com
'Effortless and fun, the new way to buy a car.' This is one of the latest services from Richard Branson's Virgin Group. You can check out any car, any time, and get advice from Quentin Willson. If you decide to order a vehicle, you can track each stage of the order and delivery process. For people who can't or don't want to wait, Virgin Cars offers Fast Track. Fast Track cars are vehicles available in the UK. They include pre-registered cars, imported cars and UK-supplied cars. Virgin says that all vehicles have a full UK specification. If you are interested in any of these Virgin will act as your agent to buy the car on your behalf. They say you won't have to wait more than 20 working days for delivery.

Fig. 79. MotorTrak has developed a very efficient car-finder service. Here it is being used to search for a secondhand BMW 328. Colour, mileage, price and location are clearly displayed.

# Motors, caravans and boats

*What Car?*

http://www.whatcar.co.uk/

This is the online version of the well-known UK magazine. There are some nice features on the site, which has a magazine feel. They can help you sell your car. The search facility on the site is good. We found a family saloon with average mileage for a very reasonable price. There is a lot of news and information here for the motorist, including reliability surveys where you can view comments about different vehicles. Whilst not scientific, it certainly made for interesting reading.

## Motoring information sites

*British Cars Web*

http://www.team.net/sol/

This is an excellent gateway site linking lots of other car sites about British cars. There are links to motoring clubs all over the world, For example, we linked to the Wolseley Car Club in Australia and were delighted to find a wonderful photo of a 1955 car, in gorgeous condition. Do visit this site, if only to view some great photos.

*BritishCar*

http://www.britishcar.com

This site is run by enthusiasts. There is an impressive number of links here, which can help any owner source parts, visit events, and find out about local clubs. We liked their fun trivia quiz, too. They say they want the site to become the most effective access point for British car information on the net.

*UK Licence Plate Information*

http://www.reg.co.uk

This is an essential site for that essential fashion accessory, the personalised number plate. Some firms seem to be buying personalised numbers to disguise the year of manufacture, since people are apt to judge the success of a business by the newness of its company vehicles. Paying thousands of pounds for special numbers can still be cheaper than replacing vehicles every year.

*Wire Wheel: UK Sports Cars*

http://www.pil.net/-mowogmg

Though possibly out of date in places, the material on the site is excellent, and well worth viewing for the brilliant photographs of some real gem condition MGs. It was surprising to discover the number of Americans with a passion for collecting British cars. If you love the traditional British sports car, you'll love this site.

*Yahoo! Cars UK*

http://cars.uk.yahoo.com/

The mighty Yahoo! internet directory offers a definitive guide to every type of car available in the UK. This is Yahoo! at its best, with an easily searchable database. We did some test searches and easily found the car specifications, current prices and photographs of the model we sought. The database also has details of UK classics. We linked to a fun site called the Cambridge Legless Frogs, a group with a love affair for the Citroen 2CV, the post war 'sardine can' that became a cultural icon.

*Yahoo! UK Automotive*
http://www.yahoo.co.uk/Recreation/Automotive/
This is another wonderful site from Yahoo!, with an obvious overlap to the one mentioned above. Once again, the site is huge, with too much to list here. It would be an essential bookmark for any motoring enthusiast.

## Car manufacturers

*Alfa Romeo*
http://www.alfaromeo.com/
OK, so their cars may be a little difficult to start at times, but the Italians certainly know how to make a sexy looking car, and Alfa are past masters at this. The site is very professionally produced and can be viewed in several languages. You can enjoy the sheer pleasure of viewing the marque, together with some of the historic posters used for marketing purposes. The site features some superb video clips and a neat calendar which you can save on your desktop.

*Aston Martin*
http://www.astonmartin.com
As one would expect from such a prestige marque, this web site is pure class. In an age of mass consumerism, it is a delight to find a manufacturer that still builds cars by hand. Aston Martin even puts the name of the craftsman who built the engine onto the engine block. Even if buying an Aston is out of your range, how about some of the merchandise – chrome wing lapel badges for example?

*BMW Cars*
http://www.bmw.co.uk/
This is the impressive web site for the UK division of the German motor manufacturer. The graphics are stunning. The pleasure of viewing cars like these is only surpassed by owning one. You can use the site to obtain literature and price lists on the range of products and services, and search from a choice of over 4,000 models to find an approved used BMW of the type you want. You can also ask for a local test drive to be arranged for you, and check out their finance packages. The site even includes a company car tax calculator.

*Citroen (France)*
http://www.citroen.com/
See Peugeot.

*Daewoo*
http://www.daewoomotor.com/
In a few years, the growth of this Korean company has been phenom-

enal. Once viewed as something of a joke, Daewoo has turned itself into an impressive global organisation. It produces affordable quality cars for the mass market and is expanding rapidly into other areas of technology. The web site is characterised by various animations, flash effects and sound tracks.

### Ferrari
http://www.ferrari.it/
This is Ferrari's official and classy-looking web site, which gives you the option of reading the information in Italian or English. The page opens with a picture of Enzo Ferrari driving a period car. It is worth visiting the site just to read the history of this extraordinary company. There is some wonderful detail on the cars accompanied by stunning photography. You can enter your name on the site and it will print out a photograph of Michael Schumacher or Eddie Irvine, with their autograph, and it will be made out to you (you'll need a colour printer). It also features a selection of electronic postcards which you can email to a friend.

### Fiat
http://www.fiat.com/
The Fiat site is available in a number of European languages. The overall design is excellent, with good quality photos that download quickly. There are also details of fan clubs on the site, and there are some nice downloadables for your desktop, if you want them. Some job opportunities are available on the site. If you are a new or recent graduate, it might be worth exploring this area. Generally this is a solid production, with some good illustration, if rather 'corporate' in tone. A more interactive approach might involve people more.

### Ford UK
http://www.ford.co.uk
Marketing executives the world over should be obliged to view this very well designed site. The opening page depicts the whole gamut of emotional experiences associated with buying a new car. This is partly what surfing is about, to help us experience the excitement of a product. The site is packed full of interest, and tells you all about the current models such as the Ka, Focus, Puma, Cougar, Escort, Mondeo and others. It also explains about Ford Direct used cars, the dealer network, environmental information and more. You can request a brochure and details of their finance packages.

### Honda
http://www.honda.com/
This is the very professional-looking web site of the major Japanese car manufacturer. There is some interesting news here about new models in the pipeline, as well as about cars already on the market. Reviewers often criticise Japanese conservative styling and dismiss their cars as being reliable but boring, but these are certainly built to quality standards and the styling is has proved popular.

*Jaguar*
http://www.jaguarcars.com/
Prepare to experience a very sophisticated site, where you will come face to face with virtual reality Jags. These web pages took a little while to download, but they are well worth the wait, especially for the new S-type. When the page downloads, you see the most beautiful representation of the car, which you can then manipulate around the screen. The site also contains details of *Sovereign* magazine. Now in Ford ownership, Jaguar's future looks very secure. Whether you are after a sports coupe or a luxury performance saloon, do visit this site. Even if a Jag is out of your range just now, there is still the pleasure of seeing how precision engineering is combined with creative design.

*Lamborghini*
http://www.lamborghini.com/
It's hard to imagine, but Lamborghini actually began by making tractors, just after the First World War. The photographs of the modern performance cars here are an absolute delight. The site is quite low on text. There is a function where you can advertise your Lamborghini for sale, but in fact the database was empty. The site gives details of their offshore activities (not tax havens, but boat racing). Lamborghini has been involved in ocean racing for ten years, and in 1994 won the World championship. This site is worth visiting, but we did feel that a marque of this quality could have done better.

*Land Rover*
http://www.landrover.com/
'The adventure starts here.' This opening message is followed by a graphic of a rugged-looking Discovery. Land Rover has built its reputation over fifty years as a maker of vehicles capable of traversing almost any terrain. The site contained details of the new Discovery, and it certainly looks as if this vehicle will keep the firm at the top. The site had some great downloads for screen savers and video clips. The clips took about 10 minutes to download but would be worth it if you are seriously interested in the product.

*Lexus*
http://www.lexus.co.uk/
The Japanese Lexus is on sale in Britain, and can be seen around quite often, though it has yet to make a breakthrough in market share. The site presents the current model range, details of the Lexus Centre Network, approved used vehicles, news, financial services, safety issues, and downloads such as the Lexus virtual showroom movie, and a screensaver. With the present bandwidth, you'll need to allow 40 to 60 minutes for these downloads.

*Maserati*
http://www.maserati.it/
This site has hardly been developed at all. Maserati has a good opening page, available in English and Italian versions, but it soon becomes clear

that the site is undeveloped and rather amateurish. We liked the cars that we could see: the 3200 GT was on show, but with only one photograph and very little background information.

Mercedes-Benz

United Kingdom

Passenger cars
Model range
Signature used cars
Mercedes Care
Dealer network

*Mercedes-Benz UK*
http://www.mercedes-benz.co.uk
As one would expect from a market leader, this is an excellent and quick-loading web site, with a delightful opening sequence of animated graphics. You will find plenty of helpful detail on all their models – the A class, C, E and S classes and sports models, as well its commercial vehicles. Mercedes have established a high international reputation, and the site mirrors the fact. To find out quickly what is available on these pages, it is worth exploring the clearly laid out site map. There is a link to Values, but you won't find used car values here, but rather a statement of the company's culture and beliefs.

*Mitsubishi*
http://www.mitsucars.com/
Mitsubishi produces some eye-catching cars. We particularly liked its concept cars on show here, the Technas in particular. Their styling is unusual, with leather and netting seats, allowing them to dry out after wet outdoor activities. They can also be folded down and used as luggage nets. The car is also fitted with satellite navigation. Mitsubishi's commitment to quality cars is clear. Like many of its competitors, it offers a downloadable screen saver, so you can place a glamorous-looking car on your desktop.

*Morgan*
http://www.morgan-motor.co.uk
The famous sport car company was formed in 1909 by HFS Morgan and has become renowned for cars of character. The Morgan may well be the last coach-built car in production, meaning that it has a self-contained steel chassis on which is mounted a wooden frame with aluminium or steel panels. The site contains plenty of detail about the models, the dealer network, and owners' clubs in the UK and elsewhere. There are the usual wallpaper downloads and screensavers, but there is a rather nice web workshop, too

*Peugeot*
http://www.psa.fr/
This is the site for the Peugeot-Citroen group from France. The design leaves something to be desired. Half of the home page was taken up with a rotating graphic, whilst the information that mattered was tucked away at the bottom. When we tried to read the history of the company, we couldn't access the promised information. The company produces some great cars but its internet presence did not seem up to speed.

*Renault*
http://www.renault.co.uk/
There is a stunning movie when you first enter the Renault site, which you

can avoid, but it is worth the wait. We also found an animated graphic of loading a van, but unfortunately could not get this to work. It kept telling us there was an error on the page. Renault has changed its image over the last thirty years from producing rather stuffy-looking vehicles to some of the most exciting yet safest cars on the roads.

*Rolls-Royce & Bentley Motor Cars*
http://www.rolls-royceandbentley.com
Here you can explore a brief history of Rolls-Royce, and the origins of the famous mascot on the cars, the Spirit of Ecstasy. There is also a longish piece about each of the Silver cars. This tradition dates back to the early days of the company when the managing director, Claude Johnson, named the first car the Silver Ghost. Since then there has been a Silver Wraith, Silver Dawn, Silver Cloud, Silver Shadow and now the Silver Seraph. The site also tells you about Bentley cars, with their more sporting tradition. The graphics download quickly and the pages are clear and easy to read.

Fig. 80. This is the clickable site map of the web site of Rolls-Royce and Bentley motor cars. It enables you to easily explore the whole range of models.

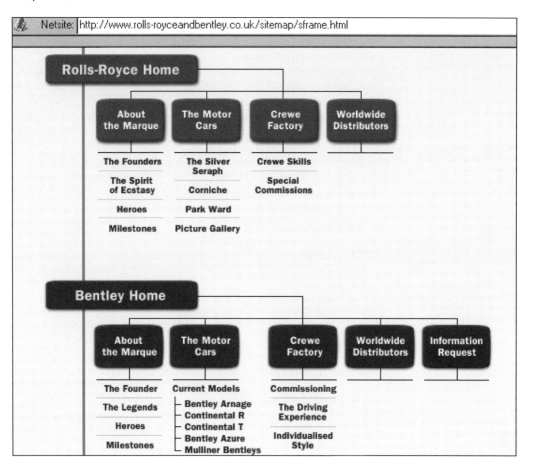

155

# Motors, caravans and boats.................................................

*Rover Cars*
http://www.rovercars.com/
Rover has been building quality cars in the UK for a very long time, and notwithstanding its recent turbulent history, the new range of products is well worth exploring, notably the 25, 45 and 75 series on which the company's future depends. The features of the site include virtual tours and a colour palette to help you choose your preferred exterior paintwork. The stylish graphics inevitably make some of the pages slow to load.

> Home

> About Us

> News

> Models

> Motorsport

> Dealers

> Merchandise

> TVR Finder

> Enquiry

*TVR Cars*
http://www.tvr-eng.co.uk/
This is the official web site of the sports car company set up in 1947 by a young engineer called Trevor Wilkinson. Its name is derived from his name, TreVoR. There are some striking-looking performance vehicles for sale on the site, and we liked the database search facility. The racing section is a must for enthusiasts, with results data available for download. You will find regional links to the dealer network, though several independent suppliers did not as yet appear to have web sites.

*Vauxhall Motors*
http://www.vauxhall.co.uk/
This is the efficient-looking site of the old-established motor manufacturer, and it promises a lot. The firm was launching a new model on the site on the day we visited, and it looked most impressive. There were some appealing interactive features. The seating concept on the new Zafira is impressive, and we liked the on-screen animation. You can also check out the current value of your own car (almost any make and model), using the on-screen service provided by Glass's Guides. You can view the latest news from Vauxhall, and explore previous stories from the last six months by clicking on Archived News. Following some disastrous placements in the JD Power and BBC *Top Gear* surveys, Vauxhall has begun to fight back.

## Retail stores

*Automobile Association*
http://www.theaa.co.uk
This is a bright, colourful easy-to-navigate site. The search engine is on the entry page, where you can enter a keyword or select a topic from a drop-down list. Contact details are also provided here. The site provides information about breakdown cover, insurance and finance, motoring and travel, news and views, and an AA bookshop. Each topic is accompanied by a short informative paragraph. The page downloads quickly and the other pages appear quickly, too, since there are relatively few graphics. This is one of the better-designed and more informative motoring sites around.

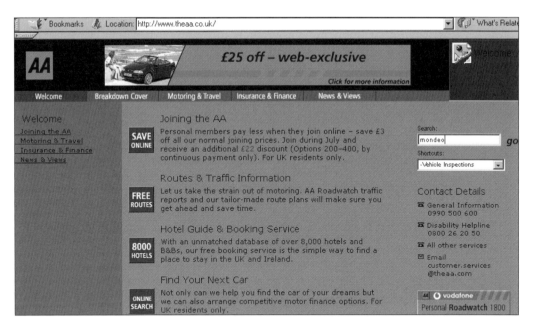

*Halfords*

http://www.halfords.co.uk

The high street retail chain Halfords has now moved online with this brightly-presented and secure virtual store. It offers a selection of top selling lines in car security, in-car entertainment, load carrying equipment, and touring and travel accessories.

Fig. 81. The web site of the AA (Automobile Association). It can help you with routes and traffic information, hotel bookings, changing your car, and motor insurance and finance.

## Caravans and caravanning

*Car-Ad*

http://www.car-ad.co.uk/

This site lists around 16,000 private and trade vehicles for sale including caravans, mobile homes, motor homes, and trailers. You can find to 2 to 8 berth vehicles, batteries, fridges, cookers, accessories, and trailers. The models include ABI, ACE, Avondale, Awning, Bailey, Compass, Conway, Crown, Eccles, Elddis, Harrison, Fairholme, Fleetwood, Lunar, Monza, Sprite, Swift and more. You can should also be able to find mobile homes of up to 40ft including Belmont, Bedford, Commer, Ford, Fiat, Mercedes, Mitsubishi, Renault, Talbot, and VW.

*The Caravan Club*

http://www.caravanclub.co.uk/

This key site is available in several languages, looking no doubt to the growth of caravanning across Europe. It has a superbly detailed database of camp sites. We checked out details of a few of these, and found the site to be well designed and illustrated, and fast to download. If you plan to venture across Europe by caravan, or just to travel within the UK, this authoritative site would be an essential bookmark.

## Boats and boating

*Norfolk Broads Yachting Co*
http://www.nbyco.com/
The Norfolk Broads Yachting Company runs the largest fleet of sailing yachts for hire on the Norfolk Broads. Its fleet offers a selection of 2 to 10 berth boats, ranging from historic gaff-rigged yachts to modern and newly built craft which provide for every comfort afloat. There are many smaller and middle range yachts, including current estuary designs, which they say are ideal for families and newcomers to the Broads.

*Sailing Now*
http://www.sailingnow.com/
This is an online magazine for sailing enthusiasts. The site includes boat and gear tests, classified advertising and crew lists, features, a forum, news and articles, harbour guides, and lots of helpful links to other sailing sites.

*Yachting.co.uk*
http://www.yacht.co.uk
Yachting.co.uk is an easy to use information resource about the UK yachting industry. You can find out about sailing clubs in the UK, weather reports, other sailing links, official sailing bodies, charts, a sailing dinghy database, and marina section.

**UK SAIL**

**Clubs**

- Abbey Sai
- Conway Ya
- Findochty
- Howth Yac
- Littlehampt
- Minnis Bay
- Nantwich &
- Penmaenn
- Rockley Cr
- Aberdeen

*UK Sailing Index*
http://www.uksail.com/
They say: 'We aim to bring you the consummate list of UK and Eire based sailing related web sites.' Here you will find hundreds of web sites of boat builders and brokers, chandlers, charters, classes, clubs, events, local information and marinas, marine services, maritime history, media, national organisations, personal pages, sailing schools and weather reports.

*Yacht Broker*
http://yacht-broker.co.uk/
The UK web site Yacht Broker provides a useful listing of yachts available from yacht brokers and private sellers. You can use the site to search for new and secondhand yachts and multihulls priced at £10,000 and above. You can search for a boat by specifying the make, price range,b length, keel type, or age of the boat you are seeking to buy. The site includes a bulletin board.

## Motorcycles

*Bikedata*
http://www.bikedata.co.uk
Bikedata offers a comprehensive directory of UK motorcycling services.

*Bike Trader*
http://www.biketrader.co.uk
Here you can search a choice of bikes throughout the UK. You can specify your search in detail, including mileage, body type and colour. You
can plan your finance options with the AA and get an insurance quote
from an insurer in its online dealer directory. Advice on buying or selling
your machine is available from leading industry brands. You can plan your
journey with RAC Traffic News, and contact the best bike web sites in
Links. The Bike Accessories area can help you out with parts, helmets
and tyres. There are directories of suppliers, and you can even bid online
in its auction store.

*BuyKawasaki*
http://www.buykawasaki.com/site/home/
This is an official US source for Kawasaki accessories, parts, clothing,
and gear.

*Car-Ad*
http://www.car-ad.co.uk/
Aside from cars, this general motoring site lists hundreds of motorcycles
for sale including Honda, Kawasaki, Suzuki, and Yamaha. You will also
find a selection of collectibles, and spares such as mudguards, fuel
tanks, wheels, tyres, exhausts, gearboxes, huggers, clothing, helmets
and boots.

*Cyberbikes*
http://www.cyberbikes.com
This enterprising site for enthusiasts offers collectable British and Italian
motorcycles from all eras. It portrays a collection of around £400,000
worth of classic and modern motorbikes offered for sale on behalf of
their owners. It has a small select collection of about 50 machines at the
moment, but hopes this number will grow. They say: 'This site relies
heavily on good quality images and inevitably there is a penalty in download times.'

*Harley-Davidson London*
http://www.harley-davidson-london.co.uk
The well-designed and illustrated site features an online store, history,
bikes and babes, sound, and animation.

*Honda Motorcycles*
http://www.hondamotorcycle.com/
Here at this US site you can increase your Honda knowledge with some
fun and interesting facts about Honda models, racing and production.

*Honda Owners Club (GB)*
http://www.hoc.org.uk

# Motors, caravans and boats......................................................

*Kawasaki GPx & GPz Owners Club*
http://www.gpxoc.force9.co.uk/gpx-index.html
The web pages here include a club history, calendar of forthcoming activities, and descriptions of past events.

*Motor Cycle News*
http://www.motorcyclenews.com/
MCN includes news and information about motorcycle products, events, and more.

*Motorbikes-Online*
http://www.motorbikes-online.co.uk/mol.asp
Here you will find a bike guide, chat, news about a range of makes, classifieds, and tyre options.

*Motorcycle World*
http://www.motorcycleworld.co.uk
The site includes various articles and reports on bike tests.

# 11 House and garden

**In this chapter we will explore:**

▶ *home furnishing*
▶ *electrical goods*
▶ *maintenance and DIY*
▶ *gardens and gardening*
▶ *buying and selling property*

## Home furnishing

This section reviews some of the UK's leading retailers and suppliers which have an online presence. Most of the major department stores are listed in chapter 5.

*Bathroom Express*
http://www.bathroomexpress.co.uk
This is a good online source of power showers, whirlpools, steam showers, pumps, taps and aromatherapy products.

*Conran Shop*
http://www.conran.co.uk/
The Conran Shop, founded by Terence Conran, opened in 1973 in the Fulham Road in London. Today its web site offers a comprehensive range of upholstered and cabinet furniture including sofas, armchairs, dining and occasional tables, chairs, storage and beds. As well as furniture, there is an extensive collection of fabrics, rugs, bed linen, cushions, blankets, lighting, glasses, jugs, bowls, stationery, shelves of vases of all

Fig. 82. Bathroom Express makes it easy to search for the fixtures and fittings you need.

shapes and colours, luggage, books, baskets, boxes and selected antiques. You will also find a bathshop, kitchenshop and childshop. There are links to dining out, as well.

*Cooks' Kitchen*
http://www.kitchenware.co.uk
The Cooks' Kitchen online kitchenware shop offers to source what you are looking for if you can't find it on the site. There's an interesting new products section, plus an 'offer of the day'. You will find kettles, teapots, plates, saucers, picnic hampers, kitchen knives and utensils, cutlery, pots, pans, chopping boards, and salt and pepper mills. The site has online ordering, but you can also order by email, post, telephone or fax if you prefer.

*David Linley & Co*
http://www.davidlinley.co.uk
This is a web site of Viscount Linley, the designer son of Princess Anne. It offers a limited but stylish collection of fine furniture and accessories in wood available from stock, but if your pocket is deep enough you also could commission items to be made for you individually,

*Fourwalls*
http://www.fourwalls.co.uk/
Fourwalls offers a large number of well organised UK-based DIY and furnishings hyperlinks for kitchen, bathroom, bedroom, living room, garden supplies. They say: 'This is the web site guaranteed to point you in the right direction in sourcing those extra touches, both big and small, that make your house a home. From fabrics, carpets and paints to beds, kitchen appliances and garden ornaments.'

*Furniture-on-Line*
http://www.furniture-on-line.co.uk/main.html
The Leeds-based Furniture-on-Line team is made up of people with experience of furniture manufacturing and retailing, new media and logistics, who felt there was a better way to shop for furniture than spending several weekends driving around from showroom to showroom. From the comfort of your home, and away from a pressured sales environment, you can explore their online showroom, and perhaps save yourself both time and money. The store offers living room furniture, kitchen and dining room furniture, children's and bedroom furniture, office furniture, music and TV units, and garden furniture.

*G-Plan Online*
http://www.morrisfurniture.co.uk/gplan/
To enter the site, the company insists that you first register your personal details. (How would you feel if you were asked for similar information before being allowed into a high street shop?) Once inside you can explore details of its various collections: Tradewinds, Fresco, Pavilion, Evolution, Visions, and Forest Springs.

*Harlequin Fabrics & Wallcoverings*
http://www.harlequin.uk.com/main.htm
Harlequin is a leading UK manufacturer of interior design products. From the comfort of your own home you can view its extensive range of fabric and wallcovering collections, to help decide the kind of colour scheme and look you want. Click on any of the thumbnail pictures to view them in full size. Some of the graphics inevitably take a little while to download. The site includes a store locator.

*Home Free*
http://www.homefree.co.uk/
Home Free offers a variety of practical and time-saving products for your home and garden. You use the web site to request its catalogue, and you can then order goods online by quoting the reference numbers. Most of the products in its range are sent direct from the supplier. If the goods you have ordered are in stock, they should arrive within ten days. When you receive your order acknowledgement you will also be issued with a sta-tionery pack explaining how to return the goods if you wish. The site uses 40-bit encryption technology. Home Free is a trading name of GUS Home Shopping Ltd.

*Home Pro*
http://www.homepro.com/
Stuck for ideas? You can start by browsing Home Pro's online magazine for ideas and inspiration on how to transform your home. Next, plan your home improvement job, using its online to form define your particular specifications and preferred timescale. This information is then matched with suitable trade professionals from the Home Pro database. Home Pro then shortlists contractors, sending them basic details for their appraisal, but withholding your name and contact details until such time as you decide to proceed.

Fig. 83. UK-based HomePro aims to help you find the tradespeople you need to complete a home improvement project.

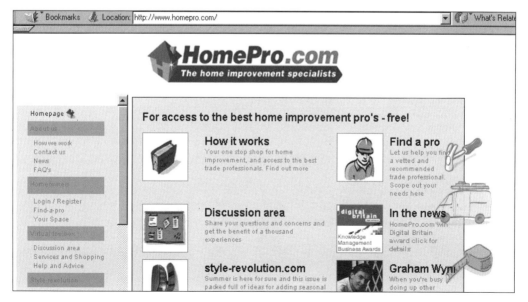

# House and garden .................................................

*Laura Ashley*
http://www.laura-ashley.com
Laura Ashley is a leading high street name in classic and modern retail fashion and home furnishings. It says it will 'shortly be launching a comprehensive online shopping catalogue.' Meantime, the web site acts as a showcase for some of its products. The site also gives details of its design service and account card, and you can request a printed catalogue from here.

*Parker Knoll*
http://www.parkerknoll.co.uk
Parker Knoll makes traditional and contemporary furniture for all areas of the home.

## Electrical goods

*Appliance Online*
http://www.applianceonline.co.uk
Here is just about everything you could ask for, including ovens, fridge-freezers, microwave ovens, hobs, dishwashers, tumble dryers and washing machines. The site offers up to 20 per cent off typical high street prices. All products are brand new and are delivered free of charge (UK mainland), fully boxed complete and with a minimum of one-year manufacturer's guarantee. It offers secure online ordering with approved SSL encryption.

*Home Electrical Direct*
http://www.hed.co.uk
The site is divided into portable TVs, video recorders, personal hi-fi, audio separates, TVs, DVD video, camcorders, in-car audio, serving trolleys,

Fig. 84. The web site of Householder Appliance Direct. As an example of the scope of its database, it offers a choice of more than 250 models of vacuum cleaner. Buying is easy when you have the right information at your fingertips.

washing machines, tumble dryers, vacuums, hi-fi systems, dishwashers, cookers, microwave ovens and refrigeration. Each category offers information on the make, model, a short description and price. There is a massive selection on all goods. There is free delivery within the mainland UK. Some of the goods have colour photos. The site is clear and easy to navigate. The order form is easy to fill and has the order number of the item already entered.

*Household Appliances Direct*
http://www.householdappliancesdirect.co.uk
The site offers a wide range of traditional white goods ranging from blenders and toasters to freezers and washing machines. The site bears the Consumer Association's Which? logo.

## Maintenance and DIY

*B & Q*
http://www.diy.co.uk
B & Q is one of Britain's top DIY and garden superstores. On its web site you can surf for products, DIY project ideas and advice, a service desk, store locations, and help. A search engine enables you to look for things by keyword, or you can choose a heading item from a drop-down list. Under products for example you can choose from adhesives, building, flooring, gardening tools and greenhouses, and many others. Practical tips are offered topics such as painting and decorating, electrical installation and repairs, fitting a front door, fitting a lock, and pruning a hedge. This is a well organised and easy to navigate site.

*DIY Books*
http://www.diybooks.co.uk
Despite the arrival of the internet, books are still a very handy store of useful information. DIY books are written by experts to help make the most of your home improvements once you have purchased the raw materials. The books cover building construction and materials, building skills, cleaning, caretaking and relocating, contracting, DIY, estimating, home furnishings and decoration, household hints, housing and property, and remodelling and renovation.

*Plumbworld*
http://www.plumbworld.co.uk
The site offers a broad range of plumbing equipment and accessories, with a 60-day money back guarantee and free delivery for most of the UK.

*Screwfix*
http://www.screwfix.com
Screwfix is the UK's largest ecommerce and mail order supplier of building, carpentry, plumbing, electrical and maintenance products. It is part of the Kingfisher retail group, which also owns Woolworths and B&Q.

*Toolfast*
http://www.toolfast.co.uk
Working on an urgent job? No time to get down to the superstore? You could use an online service like Toolfast, which offers next day delivery (mainland UK) for a range of DIY and professional products, backed by a money-back guarantee.

## Gardens and gardening

*e-Garden (UK)*
http://www.e-garden.co.uk/
Launched in 1999, this is an impressive source of advice, news, a garden events calendar, competitions and online garden shopping. It offers quality gardening journalism, images, gardening databases and e-publications. It provides a home shopping facility for plants, seeds, bulbs and other gardening products sourced from leading suppliers. The site includes a special Latin plant name translator that can change some 72,000 names from Latin to English and back again. e-Garden is the brainchild of Brian Vass, who was responsible for developing the Royal Horticultural Society web site.

*Expert Gardener*
http://www.expertgardener.co.uk
A good place to start a search would be this UK online gardening magazine, featuring Alan Titchmarsh and Charlie Dimmock. Like any gardening magazine it has regular features and articles, which you can download and print. There's a garden advice centre and a library. You can find details of products, online and email brochures from seed companies, information on specialist nurseries as well as links to other sites of interest to gardeners. These include many specialist plant societies, gardens to

Fig. 85. Expert Gardener is a must for the gardening enthusiast. It can put you in touch with fellow gardeners, as well as help you out with expert advice and tips.

visit, plant collections and other societies such as the Royal Horticultural Society.

*Garden Book*
http://www.gardenbook.com
With over 2,000 gardening titles, Garden Book claims to be the largest and most specialised bookstore for gardeners on the internet.'If we don't have it, ask. If it is anywhere, we'll find it'.

*Garden Centre*
http://www.gardencentre.co.uk/
This attractively designed web site offers seasonal tips, a diary of garden events, and links to fencing and solar fountain suppliers. It also offers 'telegardening' which it describes as the 'ultimate leisure inactivity for the committed mouse potato'. You can view, tend or water the telegarden using a robot arm with an attached video camera, all from the comfort of your favourite chair

*Garden Links*
http://www.gardenlinks.ndo.co.uk
This is a substantial directory for UK gardening suppliers, gardens to visit, advice, gardening books, wildlife gardens, garden plants and more.

*Garden Web Europe*
http://www.gardenersnet.com/index.htm
Garden Web hosts discussion forums, garden exchanges, articles, contests, a plant database, a huge garden-related glossary and online catalogues. It is home to the Calendar of Garden Events, The Rosarian, Wild Flowers and sister sites in Europe and Australia. It aims to combine interactivity with imaginative content and a user-friendly interface. Garden Web serves more than three million page views a month.

*Garden World*
http://www.gardenworld.co.uk/
This useful site covers UK garden centres, gardening topics, events, competitions, recruitment, and gardening links. With a listing of over 1,000 UK garden centres, you can explore which centres are closest to you and find out what services, facilities, plants and garden products are offered by each one. The site features various new garden products and suppliers.

*Gardening 365*
http://www.oxalis.co.uk/
This is a useful general portal site to British gardening. You can find out about plants, and gardening events in the UK, search the web, place a classified ad, or discuss gardening topics. The site includes clickable maps with dots representing gardens open to the public; click on any of these – there are hundreds – to display more detailed information.

167

# House and garden .................................................

*Gardening Launch Pad*
http://www.tpoint.net/neighbor/
This is a very enterprising and well-organised list of gardening sites all over the world. It offers more than 4,000 (mostly non-commercial) links to every imaginable aspect of gardening and horticulture. You're sure to find the answer somewhere here.

*Internet Garden*
http://www.internetgarden.co.uk/
The Internet Garden has been online for about two years, and contains a substantial number of well-organised links. It has been designed to provide a clean and simple interface, free of large image files, and with easy navigational controls. It is constantly in search of new and interesting links, so if you want to suggest a web site to add, be in touch. Well worth a look.

About Us
Events
Plants
Advice
Science
Gardens
Education
News
Join Us
e-Shop
Search

*Royal Horticultural Society*
http://www.rhs.org.uk/Around/links.asp
The RHS is Britain's largest gardening organisation. The site is easy to navigate around and from the home page you can search the RHS database to find books, plants and products. The sites listed and linked here are divided by subject into organisations, books and bookshops, colleges, gardens, individual plants and genera, societies, and magazine (general interest) sites. This is an essential bookmark for gardeners.

*Virtual Garden*
http://vg.com
This is a very substantial and useful site. 'It is created by gardeners, for gardeners. It is the place to find the inspiration and information you'll need to help you grow your garden. You can search the Time-Life Plant Encyclopedia, interact with other cyber-gardeners, gather helpful hints for your zone, and explore the world of gardening online.' Dating back to 1994, VG is one of the oldest gardening portals on the web.

*Which?Online – Gardening*
http://www.which.net/gardening/contents.html
This web site of the Consumers Association contains a whole range of products, advice, trials, tests, tips, news and ideas to help you get the most from your garden. It gives quick access to hundreds of useful gardening fact sheets and reports. Registration is required for access to parts of the site.

*Yahoo! UK Gardening*
http://uk.dir.yahoo.com/Recreation/Home.and.Garden/Gardening/
Don't forget to check out the UK gardening area of the mighty Yahoo! internet directory.

▶ *Tip* – For a comprehensive guide to this subject see *Gardens & Gardening on the Internet* by Judith & Graham Lawlor, published in the Internet Handbooks series.

## Buying and selling property

*Building Societies Association*
http://www.bsa.org.uk/
The BSA is the London-based trade association for the UK's 70 or so
building societies. Not sure where to apply for a mortgage? On the site
you will find a very handy directory of members. Societies are listed in
alphabetical order complete with head office addresses and telephone
numbers, and many now have links to their web sites.

*FIND*
http://www.find.co.uk/
FIND stands for the Financial Services Internet Directory. This excellent
site contains handy information and links to key areas of concern to
householders such as insurance, banking, investment, and financial advice.

*Find a Property*
http://www.findaproperty.com/
The site contains details of 16,000 houses and flats drawn from more
than 500 estate agents' offices. They range from studio flats to prestige
mansion homes in central London. You can search for property by following the detailed area breakdown, or enter your requirements on the
search form and retrieve a list of matching properties. You can search by
price range and general area, and even take a virtual tour of selected
homes.

Fig. 86. Find a Property is
a useful house-finding
service, which works best
for London and the home
counties. It should give
you a good idea of local
property values.

# House and garden .................................................

*French Property Owners*
http://www.french-property-owners.com/
Here is a useful resource for anyone buying, selling, renovating or letting property in France. It offers a broad of professional and business contacts – accountants, estate agents, property managers, architects, financial advisers, property search, builders, information services, removals, insurance, language courses, carpenters, lawyers, surveyors, damp proofing, plumbers, swimming pools, electricians, private letting and sales. There are articles on how to advertise the letting or sale of your property, and how to arrange security while you are away.

*Home2View*
http://www.home2view.co.uk/
The Home2View property site gives you access to the most up-to-date property search engine. Full property details for 1,000s of homes for sale with estate agents throughout Britain can be easily viewed. You can search for houses, bungalows, flats and more with its simple property search. The details are automatically updated each day.

*Home Co*
http://www.home.co.uk/
You can use Home Co to explore well over 100,000 properties, semi-detached and terraced houses, townhouses, apartments and flats, medieval castles, Tudor cottages, Edwardian villas and Victorian farm conversions. This is a residential property gateway site, containing some useful links for home buyers.

*08004homes.com*
http://www.08004homes.com/
This is an attractively presented and substantial magazine-style site which offers in-depth property-related news and features. Its database contains details of more than 70,000 properties for sale across the UK. The site is owned by Property Internet, which is run by a number of people with Fleet Street backgrounds.

*Homepages*
http://www.homepages.co.uk
Homepages offers a database of over 5,000 properties, mainly in London and the home counties. The site is refreshingly simple to navigate. Its member agencies pool their properties onto the database. You can view full details of these, or ask the agent to send them direct to you by post. The links allows you to view a map of the area, find the local schools (and even view their Ofsted reports) or find other local services.

*Homes-on-Line*
http://www.hol365.co.uk/
Homes on Line offers a functional no-frills database search for UK properties. It brings together some well-known member agencies from across the UK, including Connell, Hurford Salvi Carr, Benham & Reeves and others. Some 6,000 estate and letting agents are listed altogether. You

simply specify the area you would like your house in, the price, and the number of bedrooms required. You can hunt for houses, flats, farms and smallholdings, development land and commercial property from Antrim to Wiltshire. The database seems quite extensive.

*Internet Property Finder*
http://www.propertyfinder.co.uk/
This is a substantial UK property database covering all types of residential, business and agricultural property. With firms as well-known as Knight Frank, FPDSavills, Hamptons, General Accident, Halifax, Royal Sun Alliance and others, this is a top source of homes to buy or to rent. All details are controlled by the selling agents, and any queries have to be addressed to the agent concerned, using the button located on each property page.

*Internet Property Registry*
http://www.propreg.com/
Based in Cambridgeshire, the IPR offers a comprehensive database of UK homes, property and estate agents, with a simple search facility. It lets you browse for a home by price, location, and property type. A magazine-style section covers subjects ranging from architecture to trees, making this an information service with something extra. You can choose an architect, investigate building regulations and planning permission, energy efficiency, and the history of housing from the Iron Age. A buyer's guide explains what to look for when viewing a property.

*International Real Estate Direct*
http://www.ired.com/
This is an excellent site with links to over 115 countries, and a superb list of properties listed in each. The site offers a choice of languages as well. The site is unmissable for anyone searching for a property abroad. It has many excellent features. You can obtain information on different laws and property customs from around the world. The site also contains articles and personal experiences of people buying houses throughout the world.

*Internet French Property*
http://www.interagences-france.com/
Very up to date, this site claims to attract 10,000 visitors a week. There is an excellent reference section covering all aspects of buying a property in France – a property purchase calculator, a glossary of French legal terms, mortgage calculator, exchange rate charts, and a legal column. There are details of French public holidays, useful addresses in France, metric conversion tables, a list of French d³partements, stuff about the internet in France, vintage wine tables, tips on renovating a house, a glossary of French housing and building terms, taxation, a shopping basket calculator, and house expenses calculator.

*Loan Check*
http://www.propertymarket.co.uk/loancheck
This site asks an unsettling question: is your mortgage interest correct?

DETAIL SEARCHES
Rentals
Houses for sale
Flats for sale
International
Agricultural
Business - Leisure

OTHER ITEMS
List of agents
Regional cover
Registering
Agents info
Public info
Jobs
Contact us

According to Loan Check, an independent survey reported that 45 per cent appeared to have errors in the lenders' favour, and the errors averaged more than £1,500 on an average mortgage of £47,000. This could be a valuable service for those who feel their lender may be short-changing them.

*Money World*
http://www.moneyworld.co.uk/
This is another established and essential site for homebuyers and householders, packed full of financial resources and links for UK residents.

*National Association of Estate Agents (Property Live)*
http://www.propertylive.co.uk
This is a web site of the NAEA. It has a really comprehensive property database and web service available to both the public and estate agents. There is a colour map of the UK divided into regions. Just select the region of your choice, and view a more detailed map showing the major towns. You then click on the any of these to obtain detailed listings on the local estate agents. The screen asks you what type of agency are you interested in, and you can specify residential sales, auctions, business transfers, and commercial lettings.

*Property Point*
http://www.propertypoint.co.uk
Property Point is a very convenient point of contact if you would like to view the web sites of estate agents in just about any part of the world.

*Street Map UK*
http://www.streetmap.co.uk/
This innovative site provides address searching and street map facilities for the UK. It currently has street maps for Greater London and road atlas maps for the whole of mainland Britain. Bartholomew, through the publishers HarperCollins, supplies the geographic maps.

*UK Property Gold*
http://www.ukpg.co.uk/
UKPG is one of the largest UK property sites on the internet, with details of more than 40,000 houses, flats and other properties for sale. When we looked, the largest one advertised was 9,000 hectares including 17 farms, and the highest price was £5.5 million. They say that more than 800,000 property files are viewed every month. The site includes useful local Area Guides to 26,000 schools and colleges, recruitment agencies, around 5,000 estate agents, plus railway stations, airports and more.

*Up My Street*
http://www.upmystreet.com/
This is a fantastic site, Europe's first web site that helps you pick and probe at the latest published statistics about where you live today or might live tomorrow. Just input your post code to discover all kinds of things about the local area – property prices and trends, local schools,

**Enter Postcode**

e.g. 'N5 2PL' 

cleveland

G

Fig. 87. UK Property Gold is one of the top UK property sites on the world wide web. It also offers information on mortgages, conveyancing, insurance, area guides, and advertising.

council tax, truancy and crime rates, ambulance response times, unemployment, pollution, hospitals, doctors, dentists, cinemas and a vast amount more. There are local colour maps. You can email your MP and even check out the register of his or her financial interests in seconds. You can even search for how many bank cash machines are available locally. This innovative site is light years ahead of any other UK property site. Since its launch in 1998, it has won numerous plaudits and awards, including *Internet Magazine*'s Cool Site of the Day and the *Daily Mirror* Click of the Week. This site is unmissable for anyone thinking of moving anywhere in the UK.

▶ *Tip* – See also *Homes & Property on the Internet* by Philip Harrison, published in the Internet Handbooks series.

# Newsgroups for shoppers and traders

On Usenet, people congregate in newsgroups according to their special areas of interest. There are over 80,000 newsgroups in operation today. They range from groups created as a joke to serious-minded ones used by large groups of dedicated professionals. Almost every hobby or human interest has one or more newsgroups dedicated to it. Some newsgroups have been quiescent for years, but others generate hundreds of new posts every day.

Usenet began many years ago, long before the world wide web arrived in 1994. It started out as a communication network between universities. It was originally used to exchange information, news, and research, by linking computers to the telephone network. Now it has grown into a huge virtual international meeting place open to everyone. People all over the world can keep in contact with friends and groups of friends, discuss events, keep up with news or, indeed, talk about absolutely anything that interests them.

Here is a selection of newsgroups with opportunities to buy and sell your favourite objects. In order to access the newsgroup just type the following letters into your browser's address box (Internet Explorer, or Netscape Navigator):

news:

followed by the name of the newsgroup, for example:

news:alt.art.marketplace

Your computer should then automatically open up the newsgroup for you, so you can start reading and posting messages. It is necessary that your internet service provider (or other news server) should include the particular newsgroup in its service. Most of the well-known UK internet service providers provide a selection of 20,000 or more of the more popular newsgroups.

## Alt newsgroups

alt.art.marketplace
alt.astrology.marketplace
alt.diamonds.marketplace
alt.fitness.marketplace
alt.ham-radio.marketplace
alt.home-theater.marketplace
alt.magick.marketplace
alt.marketplace
alt.marketplace.books
alt.marketplace.books.sf
alt.marketplace.books-on-tape
alt.marketplace.cassettes
alt.marketplace.collectables
alt.marketplace.compact-disc
alt.marketplace.funky-stuff
alt.marketplace.funky-stuff.forsale
alt.marketplace.videotapes
alt.martial-arts.marketplace
alt.motorcycle
alt.motorcycles
alt.mountain-bike

alt.music.trading.dat
alt.personals.ads
alt.pets
alt.pets.arachnid
alt.pets.arachnids
alt.pets.dogs
alt.pets.ferrets
alt.pets.guinea-pigs
alt.pets.hamsters
alt.pets.hedgehogs
alt.pets.mice
alt.pets.parrots
alt.pets.parrots.marketplace
alt.pets.rabbits
alt.rock-n-roll
alt.sailing
alt.toys
alt.toys.gi-joe
alt.toys.transformers.classic.moderated
alt.toys.transformers.marketplace
alt.toys.virtual-pets
alt.trade

## Biz newsgroups

biz.marketplace
biz.marketplace.computers
biz.marketplace.computers.mac
biz.marketplace.computers.other
biz.marketplace.discussion
biz.marketplace.international
biz.marketplace.non-computer
biz.marketplace.services
biz.marketplace.services.computers
biz.marketplace.services.discussion
biz.marketplace.services.non-computer

## Comp newsgroups

comp.sys.ibm.pc.games.marketplace
comp.sys.mac.games.marketplace

## Fj newsgroups

fj.fleamarket
fj.fleamarket.appliances
fj.fleamarket.autos
fj.fleamarket.books
fj.fleamarket.books.comics
fj.fleamarket.books.comp
fj.fleamarket.books.sci
fj.fleamarket.books.soc
fj.fleamarket.comp
fj.fleamarket.misc
fj.fleamarket.tickets
fj.fleamarket.video-game

## Market newsgroups

market
market.internet
market.internet.free

## Misc newsgroups

misc.business.marketing
misc.business.marketing.moderated
misc.forsale
misc.forsale.computers
misc.forsale.computers.discussion
misc.forsale.computers.mac-specific
misc.forsale.computers.memory
misc.forsale.computers.modems
misc.forsale.computers.monitors
misc.forsale.computers.net-hardware

misc.forsale.computers.other
misc.forsale.computers.other.misc
misc.forsale.computers.other.software
misc.forsale.computers.other.systems
misc.forsale.computers.pc-specific
misc.forsale.computers.pc-specific.audio
misc.forsale.computers.pc-specific.cards
misc.forsale.computers.pc-specific.cards.misc
misc.forsale.computers.pc-specific.cards.video
misc.forsale.computers.pc-specific.misc
misc.forsale.computers.pc-specific.motherboards
misc.forsale.computers.pc-specific.portables
misc.forsale.computers.pc-specific.software
misc.forsale.computers.pc-specific.systems
misc.forsale.computers.printers
misc.forsale.computers.storage
misc.forsale.computers.workstation
misc.forsale.non-computer

## Rec newsgroups

rec.antiques.marketplace
rec.aquaria.marketplace
rec.arts.books.marketplace
rec.arts.comics.marketplace
rec.audio.marketplace
rec.autos.marketplace
rec.bicycles.marketplace
rec.boats.marketplace
rec.crafts.marketplace
rec.crafts.textiles.marketplace
rec.food.marketplace
rec.games.video.arcade.marketplace
rec.games.video.marketplace
rec.music.makers.marketplace
rec.music.marketplace
rec.music.marketplace.cd
rec.music.marketplace.misc
rec.music.marketplace.vinyl
rec.outdoors.marketplace
rec.photo.marketplace
rec.skiing.marketplace
rec.travel.marketplace
rec.video.dvd.marketplace
rec.video.marketplace

## Video newsgroups

video.laserdisc.marketplace

# My favourite bookmarks

| Name of web site (e.g. Big Shops) | Web address (e.g. http://www.bigshops.com) |
| --- | --- |
| .................................................. | .................................................. |
| .................................................. | .................................................. |
| .................................................. | .................................................. |
| .................................................. | .................................................. |
| .................................................. | .................................................. |
| .................................................. | .................................................. |
| .................................................. | .................................................. |
| .................................................. | .................................................. |
| .................................................. | .................................................. |
| .................................................. | .................................................. |
| .................................................. | .................................................. |
| .................................................. | .................................................. |
| .................................................. | .................................................. |
| .................................................. | .................................................. |
| .................................................. | .................................................. |
| .................................................. | .................................................. |
| .................................................. | .................................................. |
| .................................................. | .................................................. |
| .................................................. | .................................................. |
| .................................................. | .................................................. |
| .................................................. | .................................................. |
| .................................................. | .................................................. |
| .................................................. | .................................................. |

# Glossary of internet terms

**access provider** – The company that provides you with access to the internet. This may be an independent provider or a large international organisation such as AOL or CompuServe. See also **internet service provider**.

**Adobe Acrobat** – A type of software required for reading PDF files ('portable document format'). You may need to have Adobe Acrobat Reader when downloading large text files from the internet, such as lengthy reports or chapters from books. If your computer lacks it, the web page will prompt you, and usually offer you an immediate download of the free version.

**address book** – A directory in a web browser where you can store people's email addresses. This saves having to type them out each time you want to email someone. You just click on an address whenever you want it.

**adult check** – An age verification system that only allows the over 18s to enter adult web sites.

**affiliate programme** – A system that allows you to sell other companies products via your web site

**age verification** – Commercial systems that prevent minors from accessing adult oriented web sites

**alert** – A little piece of software that places a notice on your desktop or in your browser window, while you are online, to let you know of some relevant new piece of information on the internet.

**AltaVista** One of the half dozen most popular internet search engines. Just type in a few key words to find what you want on the internet.

**AOL** – America On Line, the world's biggest internet service provider, with more than 20 million subscribers, and now merged with Time Warner. Because it has masses of content of its own – quite aside from the wider internet – it is sometimes referred to as an 'online' service provider rather than internet service provider. It has given away vast numbers of free CDs with the popular computer magazines to build its customer base.

**applet** – An application programmed in Java that is designed to run only on a web browser. Applets cannot read or write data onto your computer, only from the domain in which they are served from. When a web page using an applet is accessed, the browser will download it and run it on your computer. See also **Java**.

**application** – Any program, such as a word processor or spreadsheet program, designed for use on your computer.

**ARPANET** – Advanced Research Projects Agency Network, an early form of the internet.

**ASCII** – American Standard Code for Information Interchange. It is a simple text file format that can be accessed by most word processors and text editors. It is a universal file type for passing textual information across the internet.

**Ask Jeeves** – A popular internet search engine. Rather than just typing in a few key words for your search, you can type in a whole question or instruction, such as 'Find me everything about online investment.' It draws on a database of millions of questions and answers, and works best with fairly general questions.

**ASP** – Active Server Pages, a filename extension for a type of web page.

**ASP** – Application Service Provider – a company that provides computer software via the internet, whereby the application is borrowed, rather than downloaded. You keep your data, they keep the program.

**attachment** – A file sent with an email message. The attached file can be anything from a word- processed document to a database, spreadsheet, graphic, or even a sound or video file. For example you could email someone birthday greetings, and attach a sound track or video clip.

**avatar** – A cartoon or image used to represent someone on screen while taking part in internet chat.

**bandwidth** – The width of the electronic highway that gives you access to the internet. The higher the bandwidth, the wider this highway, and the faster the traffic can flow.

**banner ad** – This is a band of text and graphics, usually situated at the top of a web page. It acts like a title, telling the user what the content of the page is about. It invites the visitor to click on it to visit that site. Banner advertising has become big business.

**baud rate** – The data transmission speed in a modem, measured in bps (bits per second).

**BBS** – Bulletin board service. A facility to read and to post public messages on a particular web site.

**binary numbers** – The numbering system used by computers. It only uses 1s and 0s to represent numbers. Decimal numbers are based on the number 10. You can count from nought to nine. When you count higher than nine, the nine is replaced with a 10. Binary numbers are based on the number 2: each place can only have the value of 1 or 0. You can count from nought to one.

**Blue Ribbon Campaign** – A widely supported campaign supporting free speech and opposing moves to censor the internet by all kinds of elected and unelected bodies.

**bookmark** – A file of URLs of your favourite internet sites. Bookmarks are very easily created by bookmarking (mouse-clicking) any internet page you like the look of. If you are an avid user, you could soon end up with hundreds of them! In the Internet Explorer browser and AOL they are called 'favourites'.

**Boolean search** – A search in which you type in words such as AND and OR to refine your search. Such words are called 'Boolean operators'. The concept is named after George Boole, a nineteenth-century English mathematician.

**bot** – Short for robot. It is used to refer to a program that will perform a task on the internet, such as carrying out a search.

**brokers** – Online agencies that buy and sell domain names

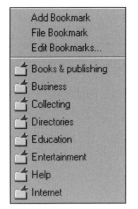

**browser** – Your browser is your window to the internet, and will normally supplied by your internet service provider when you first sign up. Itis the program that you use to access the world wide web, and manage your personal communications and privacy when online. By far the two most popular browsers are Netscape Communicator and its dominant rival Microsoft Internet Explorer. You can easily swap. Both can be downloaded free from their web sites and are found on the CD roms stuck to the computer magazines. It won't make much difference which one you use – they both do much the same thing. Other browsers include Opera and NetCaptor.

**bug** – A weakness in a program or a computer system.

**bulletin board** – A type of computer-based news service that provides an email service and a file archive.

**cache** – A file storage area on a computer. Your web browser will normally cache (copy to your hard drive) each web page you visit. When you revisit that page on the web, you may in fact be looking at the page originally cached on your computer. To be sure you are viewing the current page, press **reload** – or **refresh** – on your browser toolbar. You can empty your cache from time to time, and the computer will do so automatically whenever the cache is full. In Internet Explorer, pages are saved in the Windows folder, Temporary Internet Files. In Netscape they are saved in a folder called 'cache'.

**certificate** – A computer file that securely identifies a person or organisation on the internet.

**CGI** – Common Gateway Interface. This defines how the web server should pass information to the program, such as what it's being asked to do, what objects it should work with, any inputs, and so on. It is the same for all web servers.

**chat** – Talking to other people live online by typing into a special web page window. You can see the replies of others and take part in a group 'conversation'.

**channel (chat)** – Place where you can chat with other internet chatters. The name of a chat channel is prefixed with a hash mark, #.

**checkout** – The area of a shopping web site where you enter your credit card details, make a final check of the contents of your shopping cart, and authorise payment. The checkout area should be fully secure using state of the art encryption. Not all sites are secure, and you should approach those with caution.

**click through** – This is when someone clicks on a banner ad or other link, for example, and is moved from that page to the advertiser's web site.

**client** – This is the term given to the program that you use to access the internet. For example your web browser is a web client, and your email program is an email client.

**closed areas** – Those areas of a web site that only registered users can enter.

**colocating** – Putting your computer at another company's location so you can connect your web site permanently to the internet

**Comic Chat** – A Windows client for IRC which shows chatters as cartoon characters.

**community** – The internet is often described as a net community. This refers to the fact that many people like the feeling of belonging to a group of like-minded individuals. Many big web sites have been developed along these lines, such as GeoCities which is divided into special-interest 'neighbourhoods', or America OnLine which is strong on member services.

**compression** – Computer files can be electronically compressed, so that they can be uploaded or downloaded more quickly across the internet, saving time and money. If an image file is compressed too much, there may be a loss of quality. To read them, you uncompress – 'unzip' – them.

**content** – Articles, columns, sales messages, images, and the text of your web site.

**content services** – Web sites dedicated to a particular subject.

**cookie** – A cookie is a small code that the server asks your browser to keep until it asks for it. If it sends it with the first page and asks for it back before each other page, they can follow you around the site, even if you switch your computer off in between.

**crash** – What happens when a computer program malfunctions. The operating system of your PC may perform incorrectly or come to a complete stop ('freeze'), forcing you to shut down and restart.

**cross-posting** – Posting an identical message in several different newgroups at the same time.

**cybercash** – This is a trademark, but is also often used as a broad term to describe the use of small payments made over the internet using a new form of electronic account that is loaded up with cash. You can send this money to the companies offering such cash facilities by cheque, or by credit card. Some Internet companies offering travel-related items can accept electronic cash of this kind.

**cyberspace** – Popular term for the intangible 'place' where you go to surf – the ethereal and borderless world of computers and telecommunications on the internet.

**cybersquatting** – Using someone else's name or trademark as your domain name in the hope they will buy it from you

**cyberstalker** – An individual who pursues you or your children using email, chat rooms and newsgroups. Often attempting to arrange a meeting with children.

**cypherpunk** – From the cypherpunk mailing list charter: 'Cypherpunks assume

privacy is a good thing and wish there were more of it. Cypherpunks acknowledge that those who want privacy must create it for themselves and not expect governments, corporations, or other large, faceless organisations to grant them privacy out of beneficence. Cypherpunks know that people have been creating their own privacy for centuries with whispers, envelopes, closed doors, and couriers. Cypherpunks do not seek to prevent other people from speaking about their experiences or their opinions.'

**data** – Items of information (singular: datum). Data can exist in many forms such as numbers in a spreadsheet, text in a document, or as binary numbers stored in a computer's memory.

**dial up account** – This allows you to connect your computer to your internet provider's computer remotely.

Dial-Up
Networking

**digital** – Based on the two binary digits, 1 and 0. The operation of all computers is based on this amazingly simple concept. All forms of information are capable of being digitalised – numbers, words, and even sounds and images – and then transmitted over the internet.

**directory** – On a PC, a folder containing your files.

**DNS** – Domain name server.

**domain** – A domain is a specific area on the internet and identifies to the computers on the rest of the internet where to access particular information. Each domain has a name. The domain for Internet Handbooks for instance is: www.internet-handbooks.co.uk

**download** – 'Downloading' means copying a file from one computer on the internet to your own computer. You do this by clicking on a button that links you to the appropriate file. Downloading is an automatic process, except you have to click 'yes' to accept the download and give it a file name. You can download any type of file – text, graphics, sound, spreadsheet, computer programs, and so on.

**ebusiness** – The broad concept of doing business to business, and business to consumer sales, over the internet.

**ecash** – Short for electronic cash. See cybercash.

**ecommerce** – The various means and techniques of transacting business online.

**email** – Electronic mail, any message or file you send from your computer to another computer using your 'email client' program (such as Netscape Messenger or Microsoft Outlook).

**email address** – The unique address given to you by your ISP. It can be used by others using the internet to send email messages to you. An example of a standard email address is:

mybusiness@aol.com

**emoticons** – Popular symbols used to express emotions in email, for example the well known smiley :-) which means 'I'm smiling!' Emoticons are not normally appropriate for business communications

**encryption** – Encoding for security purposes. Email and any other data can now be encrypted using PGP and other freely available programs. Modern encryption has become so amazingly powerful as to be to all intents and purposes uncrackable. Law enforcers world wide are pressing their governments for access to people's and organisation's passwords and security keys. Would you be willing to hand over yours?

**Excite** – A popular internet directory and search engine used to find pages relating to specific keywords which you enter. See also Yahoo!.

**ezines** – The term for magazines and newsletters published on the internet.

**FAQ** – Frequently Asked Questions. You will see 'FAQ' everywhere you go on the internet. If you are ever doubtful about anything check the FAQ page, if the site has one, and you should find the answers to your queries.

**favorites** – The rather coy term for **bookmarks** – used by Internet Explorer, and by America Online.

**file** – A file is any body of data such as a word processed document, a spreadsheet, a database file, a graphics or video file, sound file, or computer program.

**filtering software** – Software loaded onto a computer to prevent access by someone to unwelcome content on the internet, notably porn. The well-known 'parental controls' include CyberSitter, CyberPatrol, SurfWatch and NetNanny. They can be blunt instruments. For example, if they are programmed to reject all web pages containing the word 'virgin', you would not be able to access any web page hosted at Richard Branson's. Virgin Net! Of course, there are also web sites that tell you step-by-step how to disable or bypass these filtering tools.

**finger** – A tool for locating people on the internet. The most common use is to see if a person has an account at a particular internet site. It is also a chat command which returns information about the other chat user, including idle time (time since they last did anything).

**firewall** – A firewall is special security software designed to stop the flow of certain files into and out of a computer network, e.g. viruses or attacks by hackers. A firewall would be an important feature of any fully commercial web site.

**flame** – A more or less hostile or aggressive message posted in a newsgroup or to an individual newsgroup user. If they get out of hand there can be flame wars.

**folder** – The name for a directory on a computer. It is a place in which files are stored.

**form** – A means of collecting data on web pages, using text boxes and buttons. For example quite a few commercial sites will ask you to register by completing an online form.

**forums** – Places for discussion on the internet. They are rather like usenet newsgroups and allow you to read, post and reply to messages. See also **bulletin board services.**

**forwarding** – Using one domain name to refer to another, like diverting your phone

**frames** – A web design feature in which web pages are divided into several areas or panels, each containing separate information. A typical set of frames in a page includes an index frame (with navigation links), a banner frame (for a heading), and a body frame (for text matter).

**freebies** – The 'give away' products, services or other enticements offered on a web site to attract registrations.

**freespace** – An allocation of free web space by an internet service provider or other organisation, to its users or subscribers.

**freeware** – Software programs made available without charge. Where a small charge is requested, the term is **shareware**.

**front page** – The first page of your web site that the visitor will see. FrontPage is also the name of a popular web authoring package from Microsoft.

**FTP** – File transfer protocol – the method the internet uses to speed files back and forth between computers. Your browser will automatically select this method, for instance, when you want to download your bank statements to reconcile your accounts. In practice you don't need to worry about FTP unless you are thinking about creating and publishing your own web pages: then you would need some of the freely available FTP software. Despite the name, it's easy to use.

**GIF** – A graphic information file. It is a compressed file format used on web pages and elsewhere to display files that contain graphic images. See also JPEG.

**graphical client** – A graphical client typically uses many windows, one for each conversation you are involved in. Each window has a command line and status bar.

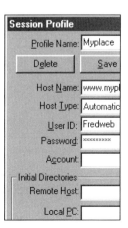

# Glossary of internet terms .............................................

**GUI** – Short for graphic user interface. It describes the user-friendly screens found in Windows and other WIMP environments (Windows, icons, mice, pointers).

**hacker** – In the sense used by the mass media, it means someone who makes or seeks to make an unauthorised entry into someone else's computer system or network. Programmers use the word hacking to refer to editing programs (hacking an unruly mess into a beautiful form, like a gardener working on a hedge). Programmers call the vandals by various other names, including 'crackers', but most of the names are unprintable.

**history list** – A record of visited web pages. Your browser probably includes a history list. It is handy way of revisiting sites whose addresses you have forgotten to bookmark – just click on the item you want in the history list. You can normally delete all or part of the history list in your browser. However, your ISP may well be keeping a copy of this information (see **internet service providers**, above).

**hit counter** – A piece of software used by a web site to publicly display the number of hits it has received.

**Hits** – The number of times a web page has been viewed.

**home page** – This refers to the index page of an individual or an organisation on the internet. It usually contains links to related pages of information, and to other relevant sites

**host** – A host is the computer where a particular file or domain is located, and from where people can retrieve it.

**HotBot** – This is a popular internet search engine used to find pages relating to any keywords you decide to enter. 'Bot' is short for robot. In internet terms it means a piece of software that performs a task on the internet, such as searching.

**HTML** – Hypertext markup language, the universal computer language used to create pages on the world wide web. It is much like word processing, but uses special 'tags' for formatting the text and creating hyperlinks to other web pages.

**HTTP** – Hyper text transfer protocol. It is the standard way that HTML documents are transferred from host computer to your local browser when you're surfing the internet. You'll see this acronym at the start of every web address, for example:

http://www.abcxyz.com

With modern browsers, it is no longer necessary to enter 'http://' at the start of the address.

**hyperlink** – See **link**.

**hypertext** – This is a link on an HTML page that, when clicked with a mouse, results in a further HTML page or graphic being loaded into view on your browser.

**IANA** – The Internet Assigned Numbers Authority, responsible for ensuring the numerical coding of the internet works

**ICANN** – The committee that oversees the whole domain name system

**Infoseek** – One of the ten most popular internet search engines.

**internet** – The broad term for the fast-expanding network of global computers that can access each other in seconds by phone and satellite links. If you are using a modem on your computer, you too are part of the internet. The general term 'internet' encompasses email, web pages, internet chat, newsgroups, and video conferencing. It is rather like the way we speak of 'the printed word' when we mean books, magazines, newspapers, newsletters, catalogues, leaflets, tickets and posters. The 'internet' does not exist in one place any more than 'the printed word' does.

**Internet II** – A new version of the internet being developed by leading academic institutions in the USA and elsewhere, intended to be restricted to educational use.

- Top of Report
- General Statistics
- Most Requested Page
- Most Submitted Form:
- Most Active Organizations
- Summary of Activity b Day
- Activity Level by Day Week
- Activity Level by Hou
- Technical Statistics

**internet account** – The account set up by your internet service provider which gives you access to the world wide web, electronic mail facilities, newsgroups and other value added

**Internet Explorer** – The world's most popular browser software, a product of MicroSoft and rival to Netscape (recently taken over by America OnLine).

**internet keywords** – A commercial service that allows people to find your domain name without having to type in www or .com

**internet protocol number** – The numerical code that is your real domain name address

**internet service providers** – ISPs are commercial, educational or official organisations which offer people ('users') access to the internet. The well known commercial ones in the UK include AOL, CompuServe, BT Internet, Freeserve, Demon and Virgin Net. Commercial ISPs may levy a fixed monthly charge, though the world wide trend is now towards free services. Services typically include access to the world wide web, email and newsgroups, as well as others such as news, chat, and entertainment. Your internet service provider will know everything you do on the internet – emails sent and received, web sites visited, information downloaded, key words typed into search engines, newsgroups visited and messages read and posted. This is why many of them are willing to offer their services free. What do they do with all this data? How long do they store it? Do they make it discreetly available to enforcement agencies? Do they allow the police private access? There are some major issues of personal privacy and data protection in all this, at both a national and European level, and state surveillance is expanding fast. At the very least, check out your service provider's privacy statement – but it may have very little value.

**intranet** – A private computer network that uses internet technology to allow communication between individuals, for example within a large commercial organisation. It often operates on a LAN (local area network).

**IP address** – An 'internet protocol' address. All computers linked to the internet have one. The address is somewhat like a telephone number, and consists of four sets of numbers separated by dots.

**IPv6** – The new internet coding system that will allow even more domain names

**IRC** – Internet relay chat. Chat is an enormously popular part of the internet, and there are all kinds of chat rooms and chat software. The chat involves typing messages which are sent and read in real time. It was developed in 1988 by a Finn called Jarkko Oikarinen.

**ISDN** – Integrated Services Digital Network. This is a high-speed telephone network that can send computer data from the internet to your PC faster than a normal telephone line.

**JavaScript** – A simple programming language that can be put onto a web page to create interactive effects such as buttons that change appearance when you position the mouse over them.

**JPEG** – The acronym is short for Joint Photographic Experts Group. A JPEG is a specialised file format used to display graphic files on the internet. JPEG files are smaller than similar GIF files and so have become ever more popular – even though there is sometimes a feeling that their quality is not as good as GIF format files. See also MPEG.

**keywords** – Words that sum up your web site for being indexed in search engines. For example for a cosmetic site the key words might include beauty, lipstick, make-up, fashion, cosmetic and so on.

**kick** – To eject someone from a chat channel.

**LAN** – Local area network, a computer network usually located in one building.

**link** – A hypertext phrase or image that calls up another web page when you click on it. Most web sites have lots of hyperlinks, or 'links' for short. These appear

183

on the screen as buttons, images or bits of text (often underlined) that you can click on with your mouse to jump to another site on the world wide web.

**Linux** – A new widely and freely available operating system for personal computers, and a potentially serious challenger to Microsoft. It has developed a considerable following.

**LINX** – The London Internet Exchange is the facility which maintains UK internet traffic in the UK. It allows existing individual internet service providers to exchange traffic within the UK, and improve connectivity and service for their customers. LINX is one of the largest and fastest growing exchange points in Europe, and maintains connectivity between the UK and the rest of the world.

**listserver** – A listserver is an automated email system whereby subscribers are able to receive and send email from other subscribers to the list.

**log on/log off** – To access/leave a network. You may be asked to 'log on' to certain sites and particular pages. This normally means entering your user ID in the form of a name and a password. In the early days of computing logging on and off literally involved writing a record in a log book.

**lurk** – The slang term used to describe reading a newsgroup's messages without actually taking part in that newsgroup. Despite the connotations of the word, it is a perfectly respectable activity on the internet.

**macros** – 'Macro languages' are used to automate repetitive tasks in Word processors.

**mail server** – A remote computer that enables you to send and receive emails. Your internet access provider will usually act as your mail server.

**mailing list** – A forum where messages are distributed by email to the members of the forum. The two types of lists are discussion and announcement. Discussion lists allow exchange between list members. Announcement lists are one-way only and used to distribute information such as news or humour. A good place to find mailing lists is Listz (http://www.liszt.com). You can normally quit a mailing list by sending an email message to request removal.

**marquee** – A moving (scrolling) line of text on a web site, normally used for advertising purposes.

**media player** – Software on a personal computer that will play sounds and images including video clips and animations.

**metasearch engine** – A site that sends a keyword search to many different search engines and directories so you can use many search engines from one place.

**meta tags** – The technical term for the keywords used in your web page code to help search engine software rank your site.

**modem** – This is an internal or external piece of hardware plugged into your PC. It links into a standard phone socket, thereby giving you access to the internet. The word derives from MOdulator/DEModulator.

**moderator** – A person in charge of a mailing list, newsgroup or forum. The moderator prevents unwanted messages.

**MPEG** – The file format used for video clips available on the internet. See also JPEG.

**MP3** – An immensely popular audio format that allows you to download and play music on your computer. See http://mpeg.org for further technical information, or the consumer web site www.mp3.com.

**MUDs** – Multi-User Dungeons, interactive chat-based fantasy world games. Popular in the early days of the internet, they are in now in decline with the advance of networked arcade games such as Quake and Doom.

**multi-phased medium** – The internet is a multi-phased medium. In other words, it can be used in many different ways to do many different things.

**navigate** – To click on the hyperlinks on a web site in order to move to other web pages or internet sites.

**Net** – A slang term for the internet. In the same way, the world wide web is often

Getting Started

My.MP3
MP3.com Mess
Store - Free Extr

Free Music

just called the web.

**metiquette** – Popular term for the unofficial rules and language people follow to keep electronic communication in an acceptably polite form.

**Netmeeting** – This Microsoft plugin allows a moving video picture to be contained within a web page. It is now integrated into Windows Media Player.

**Netscape** – After Internet Explorer, Netscape is the most popular browser software available for surfing the internet. An excellent browser, Netscape has suffered in the wake of the rise of Microsoft's Internet Explorer, mainly because of the success of Microsoft in getting it pre-loaded on most new PCs. Netscape Communicator comes complete with email, newsgroups, address book and bookmarks, plus a web page composer, and you can adjust its settings in all sorts of useful ways. Netscape was taken over by American Online for $4 billion.

**nettie** – Slang term for someone who likes to spend a lot of time on the internet.

**newbie** – Popular term for a new member of a newsgroup or mailing list.

**newsgroup** – A Usenet discussion group. Each newsgroup is a collection of messages, usually unedited and not checked by anyone ('unmoderated'). Messages can be placed within the newsgroup by anyone including you. It is rather like reading and sending public emails. The ever-growing newsgroups have been around for much longer than the world wide web, and are an endless source of information, gossip, news, entertainment, sex, politics, resources and ideas. The 50,000-plus newsgroups are collectively referred to as Usenet, and millions of people use it every day.

**newsreader** – A type of software that enables you to search, read, post and manage messages in a newsgroup. It will normally be supplied by your internet service provider when you first sign up, or preloaded on your new computer. The best known are Microsoft Outlook, and Netscape Messenger.

**news server** – A remote computer (eg your internet service provider) that enables you to access newsgroups. If you cannot get some or any newsgroups from your existing news server, use your favourite search engine to search for 'open news servers' – there are lots of them freely available. When you have found one you like, add it to your news reader by clicking on its name. The first time you do this, it may take 10 to 20 minutes to load the names of all the newsgroups onto your computer, but after that they open up in seconds whenever you want them.

**nick** – Nickname, an alias you can give yourself and use when entering a chat channel, rather than using your real name.

**Nominet** – The official body for registering domain names in the UK (for example web sites whose name ends in .co.uk).

**online** – The time you spend linked via a modem to the internet. You can keep your phone bill down by reducing online time. The opposite term is offline.

**op** – A chat channel operator.

**open source software** – A type of freely modifiable software. A definition and more information can be found at: www.opensource.org

**OS** – The operating system in a computer, for example MS DOS (Microsoft Disk Operating System), or Windows 95/98.

**packet** – Term for a small piece of data sent or received over the internet on your behalf by your internet service provider, and containing your address and the recipient's address.

**ParaChat** – ParaChat offers Java-based web chat rooms to any webmaster who wants to use it.

http://www.parachat.com/

**parking** – Placing your domain into storage until you want to use it at a later date

**PC** – Personal computer.

**ping** – You can use a ping test to check the connection speed between your computer and another computer.

**online** – Being connected to the internet.

**Pentium** – The name of a very popular microprocessor chip in personal computers. The first Pentium IIIs were supplied with secret and unique personal iden-
tifiers, which ordinary people surfing the net were unwittingly sending out,
enabling persons unknown to construct detailed user profiles. After a storm
of protest, Pentium changed the technology so that this identifier could be
disabled. If you buy or use a Pentium III computer you should be aware of this
risk to your privacy when online.

**PGP** – Pretty Good Privacy. A method of encoding a message before transmitting it over the internet. With PGP, a message is first compressed then en-
coded with the help of keys. Just like the valuables in a locked safe, your
message is safe unless a person has access to the right keys. Many governments (as in France today) would like complete access to people's private
keys. New Labour wanted access to everyone's keys in the UK, but dropped
the proposed legislation after widespread protests. Unlike in many countries,
there is no general right to privacy in the UK.

**plugin** – A type of (usually free and downloadable) software required to add
some form of functionality to web page viewing. A well-known example is
Macromedia Shockwave, a plugin which enables you to view animations.

**plugin chat** – A form of internet chat which depends on your downloading and
installing additional software for your web browser.

**PoP** – Point of presence. This refers to the dial up phone numbers available from
your ISP. If your ISP does not have a local point of presence (i.e. local access
phone number), then don't sign up – your telephone bill will rocket because
you will be charged national phone rates. All the major ISPs have local numbers covering the whole of the country.

**portal site** – Portal means gateway. A portal site includes the one that loads into
your browser each time you connect to the internet. It could for example be
the front page of your internet service provider. Or you can set your browser
to make it some other front page, for example a search engine such as Yahoo!,
or even your own home page if you have one.

**post, to** – The common term used for sending ('posting') messages to a newsgroup. Posting messages is very like sending emails, except of course that
they are public and everyone can read them. Also, newsgroup postings are archived, and can be read by anyone in the world years later. Because of this,
many people feel more comfortable using an 'alias' (made-up name) when
posting messages.

**privacy** – You have practically no personal privacy online. Almost every mouse
click and key stroke you make while online is being electronically logged, ana-
lysed and possibly archived by internet organisations, government agencies,
police or other surveillance services. You are also leaving a permanent trail of
data on whichever computer you are using. But then, if you have nothing to
hide you have nothing to fear. To explore privacy issues worldwide visit the
authoritative Electronic Frontier Foundation web site at www.eff.org, and for
the UK, www.netfreedom.org.

**protocol** – A set of rules. Technical term for the method by which computers
communicate. A protocol is something that has been agreed and can be used
between systems. For example, for viewing web pages your computer would
use hypertext transfer protocol (http). For downloading and uploading files, it
would use file transfer protocol (ftp).

**proxy** – An intermediate computer or server, used for reasons of security.

**Quicktime** – A popular free software program from Apple Computers that will
play sounds and images including video clips and animations on both Apple
Macs and personal computers.

**rank** – Your place on the list of web sites produced by a search engine, as a result of someone doing a search.

**real-time web chat** – Form of chat in which a web page is continually reloaded. You can only see the last few lines of the conversation at any one time.

**refresh, reload** – The refresh or reload button on your browser toolbar tells the web page you are looking at to reload.

**register** – You may have to give your name, personal details and financial information to some sites before you can continue to use the pages. Site owners may want to produce a mailing list to offer you products and services. Registration is also used to discourage casual traffic.

**registered user** – Someone who has filled out an online form and then been granted permission to access a restricted area of a web site. Access is usually obtained by logging on, in other words entering a password and user name.

**search engine** – A search engine is a web site you can use for finding something on the internet. Popular search engines are big web sites and information directories in their own right. There are hundreds of them; the best known include Alta Vista, Excite, Google, Infoseek, Lycos and Yahoo!.

**secure servers** – The hardware and software provided so that people can use their credit cards and leave other details without the risk of others seeing them online. Your browser will tell you when you are entering a secure site.

**secure sockets layer (SSL)** – A standard piece of technology which ensures secure financial transactions and data flow over the internet.

**security certificate** – Information that is used by the SSL protocol to establish a secure connection. Security certificates contain information about who it belongs to, who it was issued by, some form of unique identification, valid dates, and an encrypted fingerprint that can be used to verify the contents of the certificate. In order for an SSL connection to be created both sides must have a valid security certificate.

**server** – Any computer on a network that provides access and serves information to other computers.

**shareware** – Software that you can try before you buy. Usually there is some kind of limitation to the game such as a time limit, or limited features. To get the registered version, you must pay for the software, typically $20 to $40. A vast amount of shareware is now available on the internet.

**Shockwave** – A popular piece of software produced by Macromedia, which enables you to view animations and other special effects on web sites. You can download it free and in a few minutes from Macromedia's web site. The effects can be fun, but they slow down the speed at which the pages load into your browser window.

**shopping agent** – The internet term for a web site or piece of software called a 'bot' that acts as a search engine, looking for the best deal on a particular product or service.

**shopping basket (or shopping cart)** – The internet term for the place where you store details of the goods you wish to purchase. You can normally view the contents of your shopping basket at any time, and add to, or delete, the contents before you enter the online checkout (payment) area.

**signature file** – This is a little computer text file in which you can place your address details, for adding to email and newsgroup messages. Once you have created a signature file you can append it to your emails as often as you like.

**Slashdot** – One of the leading technology news web sites, found at: http://slashdot.org

**smiley** – A form of **emoticon**.

**snail mail** – Popular term for the standard postal service involving post-persons, vans, trains, planes, sacks and sorting offices.

# Glossary of internet terms ...........................................

**sniffer** – A program on a computer system (often an ISP's system) designed to collect information about people using the internet. Sniffers are often used by hackers to collect passwords and user names, or by surveillance agencies to track activity on the internet.

**spam** – The popular term for electronic junk mail – unsolicited and unwelcome email messages sent across the internet. The term comes from Monty Python. There are various forms of spam-busting software which you can now obtain to filter out unwanted email messages.

**subscribe** – The term for accessing a newsgroup in order to read and post messages in the newsgroup. There is no charge, and you can subscribe, unsubscribe and resubscribe at will with a click of your mouse. Unless you post a message, no-one in the newsgroup will know that you have subscribed or unsubscribed.

**surfing** – Slang term for browsing the internet, especially following trails of links on pages across the world wide web.

**sysop** – Systems operator, someone rather like a moderator for example of a chat room or bulletin board service.

**Talk** – A form of internet chat, less used today. It was succeeded by Ntalk ('new talk') with which it was incompatible.

**talkers** – Servers which give users the opportunity to talk to each other. You connect to them, take a 'nickname' and start chatting. Usually, they offer some other features besides just allowing users to talk to each other, including Bulletin Boards, a 'world' such as a city or building, which you move around in. an opportunity to store some information on yourself, and some games.

**TCP/IP** – Transmission Control Protocol/Internet Protocol, the essential technology of the internet. It's not normally something you need worry about.

**telnet** – Software that allows you to connect via the internet to a remote computer and work as if you were a terminal linked to that system.

**textual client** – Textual clients run on a text screen (or window). They split it into a one-line command line at the bottom, a status bar just above that, and a chat message window in the rest of the screen.

**theme** – A term in web page design. A theme describes the general colours and graphics used within a web site. Many themes are available in the form of readymade templates.

**thread** – An ongoing topic in a usenet newsgroup or mailing list discussion. The term refers to the original message on a particular topic, and all the replies and other messages which spin off from it. With news reading software, you can easily 'view thread' and thus read the related messages in a convenient batch.

**top level domain** – The last code in the domain name, such as .com or .uk

**traceroute** – A program that traces the route from your machine to a remote system. It is useful if you need to discover a person's ISP, for example in the case of a spammer.

**traffic** – The amount of data flowing across the internet, to a particular web site, newsgroup or chat room, or as emails.

**trojan horse** – A program that seems to perform a useful task but is really a malevolent program designed to cause damage to a computer system.

**uploading** – The act of copying files from your PC to a server or other PC on the internet, for example when you are publishing your own web pages. The term is most commonly used to describe the act of copying HTML pages onto the internet via FTP.

**UNIX** – This is a computer operating system that has been in use for many years, and still is used in many larger systems. Most ISPs use this operating system.

**URL** – Uniform resource locator – the address of each internet page. For instance the URL of Internet Handbooks is http://www.internet-handbooks.co.uk

**Usenet** – The collection of well over 80,000 active newsgroups that make up a substantial part of the internet.

**virtual reality** – The presentation of a lifelike scenario in electronic form.

**virtual server** – A portion of a PC that is used to host your domain

**virus** – A computer program maliciously designed to cause havoc to people's computer files. Viruses can typically be received when downloading program files from the internet, or from copying material from infected disks. Even Word files can now be infected. You can protect yourself from the vast majority of them by installing some inexpensive anti-virus software, such as Norton, McAfee or Dr Solomon.

**WAP** – Wireless application protocol, a technology that enables the internet to be accessed by mobile phones, palm pilots and others PDAs (personal data assistants).

**web authoring** – Creating HTML pages to upload onto the internet. You will be a web author if you create your own home page for uploading onto the internet.

**Webcrawler** – A popular internet search engine used to find pages relating to specific keywords entered.

**webmaster** – Any person who manages a web site.

**web pages** – Individual sets of information that can be viewed completely on one screen (though you may need to scroll down to see the whole page)

**web rings** – A network of interlinked web sites that share a common interest.

**web site** – a set of web pages which are interconnected

**WHOIS** – A database of domain name registry information

**Windows** – The hugely popular operating system for personal computers developed by Bill Gates and the Microsoft Corporation. The Windows 3.1 version was followed by Windows 95, further enhanced by Windows 98 and now Windows 2000.

**Write** – A chat program called Write flashes a message on the screen of another user, named on the command line. The other user can then use the same command to write on the screen of the first user. By agreeing a few simple rules, it's possible to hold a workable conversation with another user.

**WWW** – The world wide web. Since it began in 1994 this has become the most popular part of the internet. The web is now made up of more than one billion web pages of every description, typically linking to other pages. Developed by a British computer scientist, Tim Berners-Lee, its growth has been exponential and is set to continue so.

**WYSIWYG** – 'What you see is what you get.' If you see it on the screen, then it should look just the same when you print it out.

**Yahoo!** – Still the world's biggest and most popular internet directory and search engine, and now valued on Wall Street at billions of dollars.

**zip/unzip** – Many files that you download from the internet will be in compressed format, especially if they are large files. This is to make them quicker to download. These files are said to be zipped or compressed. Unzipping these compressed files generally refers to the process of returning them to their original size on receipt. Zip files have the extension '.zip' and are created (and unzipped) using WinZip or a similar popular software package.

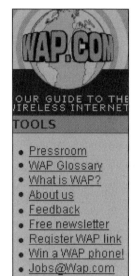

WAP.COM

OUR GUIDE TO THE WIRELESS INTERNET

TOOLS

- Pressroom
- WAP Glossary
- What is WAP?
- About us
- Feedback
- Free newsletter
- Register WAP link
- Win a WAP phone!
- Jobs@Wap.com
- Advertise?

# Index

# Index ...........................................................